the
**UPPERCASE**
# COMPENDIUM
*of*
**CRAFT & CREATIVITY**

# THE COMPENDIUM OF

# CRAFT AND CREATIVITY

*compiled by*

# UPPERCASE

*the quarterly print magazine
for the creative and curious*

*Thank you to the makers and their photographer friends for providing the images that appear in this book.*

**UPPERCASE PUBLISHING INC**
201b – 908, 17th Ave SW
Calgary, Alberta, Canada  T2T 0A3
**uppercasemagazine.com**

**WRITING** Janine Vangool & Glen Dresser
**DESIGN** Janine Vangool / UPPERCASE
**COPYEDITING** Correy Baldwin
**PRINTED IN CANADA** The Prolific Group

To my creative
and curious Finley,
♥ always.

# INTRODUCTION

I'm a maker. It just so happens that I make books and magazines. Whether through UPPERCASE magazine or my other publications, my goal is to uplift my readers—to share your stories, to inspire you—and also to express myself through the design and creation of a printed artifact.

Within the print industry, there is a long tradition of publishing creative annuals. Graphic design, illustration and advertising each have their various annual books and special edition magazines that compile the best of each category. For designers and illustrators, to be included in an annual is a benchmark of success. It helps get them recognized within their industry and opens doors to new opportunities. For aspiring creatives, annuals showcase what is possible in a given field. These books inspire, educate and promote. And as the years pass, the annuals serve as important cultural artifacts—a snapshot of the trends and aesthetics of a particular year.

When it comes to craft and the independent maker movement, however, there is no annual to celebrate and document all the amazing talent and beautiful products being made each year. Across the Internet there are blog posts, websites and Etsy listings, but these are scattered and fleeting: items are sold, sites are updated with more current projects and blog posts quickly get buried by the latest thing. We're so busy looking for what's new that there isn't time to appreciate what we've already done.

This first edition of the UPPERCASE Compendium of Craft & Creativity is an artifact of the flourishing handmade and creativity movement. Within, you'll discover inspiring makers, crafters and artists. You'll find out how—and why—they do what they do.

And, if I've done my job right, you just might find a little bit of yourself in these pages. My hope is that these stories and gorgeous images ignite the creative spark that exists within you—within all of us.

*Janine Vangool*

**PUBLISHER / EDITOR / DESIGNER**
*janine@uppercasemagazine.com*
*uppercasemagazine.com*

RICHARD GARY

# THE MAKERS

# SHASTA GARCIA

SAN FRANCISCO,
CALIFORNIA, USA

When she's not at her full-time graphic design job or volunteering with the San Francisco chapter of the AIGA (American Institute of Graphic Arts), you can find Shasta Garcia making things either in her second bedroom studio or in her garage.

"I have a small tabletop letterpress on wheels in my garage stored next to a washer/dryer," she says. "I move my car when I want to use the space for printing. For larger printing projects I reach out to my larger printing community as a resource."

She makes cat toys, paper flowers and greeting cards using paper arts, calligraphy, letterpress and needle felting—the exploration of the medium is as important as what she creates. "I think of my work as being designed with craft," Shasta explains. "It is unique because I put a twist on recognizable objects or craft materials. Instead of trying to compete with all the wonderful letterpress greeting cards on

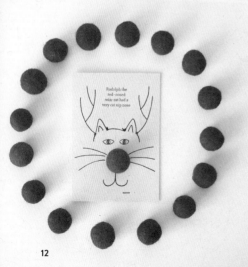

Rudolph the
red-nosed
rein-cat had a
very cat nip nose

the market, I try to use letterpress to create products I've never seen before." For example, Kitty ConfetTea is a tea (for humans) made of 50 percent catnip, as well as hibiscus, sunflower petals, carrot and green rooibos. The tea is for humans as well as their cats: "A muslin confetti printed bag is included for making a toy for your kitty out of the dry tea. The images on the side of the box show a little story of how cats get amped up when exposed to catnip and then shortly after crash out into a nap."

"Putting a twist on the use of materials has led me create many cat toys, and though I'm a little wary of the term I am starting to be called 'the cat lady' at craft events. When not being called a cat lady I'm called a 'wrapper.' When I first started my blog I shared mostly imagery of gifts I'd wrapped. This led to being one of eight contestants in the Scotch Most Gifted Wrapper contest in 2012."

Shasta has always been interested in art and making. "I remember developing my fine motor skills with origami at an early age," she says. "I've come to find it's important to acknowledge that I grew up an only child. This created independence and the ability to keep myself entertained. So although I am naturally an extrovert, years of solitude also cultivated a need for introversion to feel balanced, and naturally during those moments I make."

With other crafters and makers sharing their work online, trends and fashions start to emerge. Shasta pays attention to what's happening and popular, and uses this as inspiration to experiment: "I do think there is a trend for products that feel handmade or have a human quality to them, especially for gift giving. I definitely like to explore trending craft mediums, such as calligraphy and weaving, to see if something can be relevant for my design work."

"The process that does connect them all is play. The majority of my projects involve paper of some sort, so that is usually the fundamental element I'm playing with. Playing with materials often brings a creative spark to make something specific. Or sometimes I make a gift for someone and realize it would be a product of interest to others." Shasta has noticed that not all inspiration comes from stimulating input. "Sometimes the creative spark even comes from boredom while retouching photographs," she says.

"I know my work will evolve—the only thing I am certain of is that I will seek creative outlets that keep me enlivened and excited."

- **WEBSITE** *shastablasta.com*
- **SHOP** *shastablasta.etsy.com, kittyconfetti.etsy.com*
- **TWITTER** *@shasta_blasta*
- **INSTAGRAM** *@shastablastawraps*

# CECILLE CASWELL

### SHERWOOD PARK, ALBERTA, CANADA

Although the art classes that Cecille Caswell found herself enrolled in from childhood rarely excited her, she nonetheless now finds herself leading an extremely prolific creative life. For this, she has another generation to thank: her mother was a dressmaker who loved fabric and colour, and her mother-in-law encouraged her in other textile arts, including knitting, quilting and, finally, rug hooking. It is this last discipline for which Cecille has a creative passion.

She sees herself as part of a growing collection of rug hookers who are deviating from patterns and coming up with their own designs, dyeing wool and creating work that is unique to them. She is obsessive about colour, which she attributes to her mother's influence. "I am passionate about colour," she says. "My house is full of it. I began to dye my own wool when I wasn't able to find the bright colours I love." Her basement contains not only a sewing room

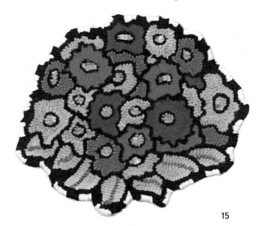

The results are designs that burst with colour—bright tapestries of her life's passions: bold floral patterns, compelling portraits, food, even dogs, often surrounded by equally striking borders, sometimes abstract and sometimes concrete. These works find an audience through craft fairs, Etsy and word of mouth, though she has also found a market for her custom dyeing work and teaches rug-hooking camps. She is also the president of a rug-hooking guild in Edmonton, which meets monthly, offers classes and support for new members and has a store that sells supplies. She also meets with a more intimate group of about 10 friends. The challenges that she works on with these friends provide a source of inspiration, but they certainly are not her only source. She also finds inspiration in "visiting art galleries and shops, magazines, books, cards, nature, doing art with grandchildren, brainstorming with friends, photos, street art, spending time with other creative people, teaching, dyeing and knitting."

but a dye kitchen that her husband built for her. These two rooms are generally messy and cluttered: "Until I reach a state of agitation, which prompts me to organize. As I'm doing so, new ideas may inspire me."

For Cecille, projects start with sketching or writing down ideas, even awakening in the night to jot them down. "I make a few templates to get the design down on linen with a felt pen," she explains. "I rarely start with a complete design because I make many changes as I go. Then I get into my stash to find the colours that may interest me. I often will dye the wool to produce the colours I need. Once these basic requirements are done, I begin to hook and rip and hook and rip until I am satisfied with my piece."

But, appropriate for someone who learned her craft from family, it is still family that provides one of her strongest motivations: "My sister and I live many miles apart and have an ongoing travelling art project. We add to it, then mail it back and forth until we feel that it is complete and start another."

• WEBSITE *edmontontraditionalrughookersguild.com*

> *"After having spent time pursuing another profession, I can honestly say I am not myself when I am not making. To create is to breathe. I know that now."*

LISA ANDERSON
SHAFFER

# LISA ANDERSON SHAFFER

FAIRFAX, CALIFORNIA, USA

"I was the kid that everyone else knew was going to be an artist before I even did," recounts Lisa Anderson Shaffer. "From the time I was small I was always making and doing. Whether it was clay or crayons, I was a nonstop creativity machine. Up until I was in my late 20s I never wanted to be anything else but an artist."

"And then surprisingly, after an artist in residency at UCSF Cancer Center, I found myself deeply interested in psychology. I returned to school to receive a master's in clinical psychology and became a psychotherapist in private practice. I thought I was happy and fulfilled, but ended up not making a single piece of art for six years—a sure sign that something was wrong. After a chaotic year full of family tragedy and celebration, I decided to leave my practice and return to teaching fine art."

Lisa began Zelma Rose while pregnant with her daughter. "For the first two years of life it was a wait-and-see hobby that was slowly turning into a business," she says. "Now, five years later it has blossomed into the business I've always dreamed of. Always full of surprises, excitement, and ups and downs, this creative life is the one I was meant to lead." Under the brand Zelma Rose, Lisa makes hand-stitched goods for men, women and the home. "I am best known for my hand-stitched necklaces," she says, "specifically my Zodiac Constellation Collection."

Working from a beautiful home studio atop a mountain in Fairfax, California, Lisa watches the sun rise over the mountain through giant pine trees that grow on their property. "I work from two desks, a sewing table and a shipping centre, and try to move around as much as possible," she says. "On my desk you will find my grandmother Zelma's collection of scissors and my grandfather Kingston's wooden ruler. I use them both every single day."

"When I sit down in my studio to design for Zelma Rose, I reference a kaleidoscope of ideas and images. As an artist, I am a hunter and a gatherer—a visual editor, a collector, a cultivator and a farmer of ideas and design. Sometimes a design will come to fruition in a single afternoon, other times it is the careful cultivation of successes and failures over the span of a year." Lisa loves when something just clicks: "Moments like that

feel magical and remind me how much I love the mystery of the artistic process." Thinking in words rather than pictures, Lisa does not typically sketch her designs. From notes she goes straight into a prototype. "By listening to the materials and responding to what they are doing I always end up going somewhere a little bit different then I had imagined. It's exciting, challenging and feels genuine."

Her business continues to grow year after year. Through Etsy, craft fairs and a wholesale rep who sells to brick-and-mortar stores, Zelma Rose is getting out into the world. "I'm a big believer in the idea that we don't get time back, so be in that time," says Lisa. "Whether it is moving too fast or too slow, be in it, process it and learn from it. Once it passes, it's over. I have goals for my business to grow in directions I never would have imagined, like books and product styling. The years ahead include work with fine metals and the continuation of constantly refining my designs."

"Letting go of the fear that I will never have a creative thought or idea again has been huge. I've been at this game for long enough to know that I simply don't have to worry about that." Lisa has advice that universally applies to all artists: "Ideas come and go all the time. Inspiration is everywhere. Open your mind, look and listen."

- **WEBSITE/SHOP** *zelmarose.com*
- **BLOG** *zelmarose.blogspot.com*
- **TWITTER** *@ZelmaRoseCurios*
- **INSTAGRAM** *@zelmarose*

# ANNIE CHEN

VANCOUVER,
BRITISH COLUMBIA, CANADA

Annie Chen makes kitchen linens, fabric storage baskets, canvas bags and paper products decorated with her surface pattern designs under her company name Lemonni. "I like to use simple shapes and unconventional colour combinations in my design," she says.

Annie observes people and objects in her everyday environment, carrying a notebook in which to sketch and jot down ideas. Sometimes the simplest thing, like an acorn, can inspire a fabric. "I try to travel or visit galleries and shows as much as I can to stay inspired," she says. "Believe it or not, going shopping motivates me, because whenever I see something beautiful I think, I want to make that, too." She digitizes her favourite sketches to begin the process of designing repeats. "Sometimes I like to add a bit of texture by drawing my graphics with watercolour or colour pencils, and then scanning them into the computer."

23

> *"I'm passionate about my work because I get to do what I love doing— designing and creating."*
>
> ANNIE CHEN

Annie was born in Taiwan and moved to Canada as a teenager. "Ever since I was a kid, I have been collecting beautiful letterheads, paper and packaging. Sometimes my parents thought I was collecting garbage, but I think I was just trying to appreciate art and design." She studied biochemistry and psychology in school, but after travelling and working abroad in London, she was inspired to pursue a creative path. "I started to freelance as a graphic designer and take some relevant courses along the way."

Intimidated at first by sourcing materials and the startup costs, it took Annie a while before she decided to turn her designs into a commercial venture. Now that she has been selling her goods for a few years through venues like Etsy, local craft fairs and her own retail location, she has a new perspective: "Selling my products

has helped push my creativity. I'm passionate about my work because I get to do what I love doing—designing and creating."

From managing her own retail and production, Annie is familiar with the delicate balance of doing things herself and knowing when to outsource: "I have learned that I should focus on what I do best and to delegate to others when it gets busier. It is easy to fall into the trap if I try to get everything perfect as well as micromanage everything. It could take forever to make every little detail perfect, and I could lose focus." She makes her own textiles and paper lines, but for more complex sewn goods she gets outside help.

"My brand is fairly new and there's a lot that I'm still learning and figuring out. I just feel that I'm really blessed to be able to pursue what I love, and to have tons of support from my family and friends," she says. Sharing a studio with her husband, a photographer, has been a great benefit: "He has been encouraging me to pursue my dream right from the start," says Annie. Together, they have a small showroom at the front of their studio. "Occasionally we team up with our friends and organized a pop-up shop in the space. We have met a lot of creative professionals living in our community because of the storefront, and our neighbours seem to appreciate a space like this."

Having firsthand encounters with customers and being able to market-test a new product in a retail environment is valuable as well: "Although I'm creating what I love, I also need to determine what the market might like and if the product will do well in that category. Sometimes the work that I'm most proud of isn't necessarily the most popular. It's always a challenge to create something that's in trend while still keeping my unique style."

- **WEBSITE** *lemonni.com*
- **TWITTER** *@lemonni*
- **INSTAGRAM** *@lemonni*

# ANGELA MCGRATH

## VANCOUVER, BRITISH COLUMBIA, CANADA

"Epoché is a line of high-quality vegetable-tanned leather goods that are hand stitched and hand printed," says Angela McGrath about her fashion accessories brand.

"It pulls together inspiration from painting, printmaking, pattern design and studies in contemporary culture; the result is a merging of fine art with fashion. The objective of Epoché is to create modern and sophisticated designed bags that also allow for a sense of personal artistic expression to be infused into the everyday."

Her bags, wallets and backpacks are the antithesis of disposable fashion, with the vegetable-tanned leather (which has no harsh chemicals or synthetic finishes) meant to age beautifully. The bags are constructed by hand, stitched with waxed linen thread. The leather, imported from Italy, is an expensive material that leaves little room for mistakes. This challenges Angela to approach her work in a very studied way: "There is something about working within the limitations of leather that really excites and challenges me. New techniques are balanced by traditional methods, and each move affects the next, forcing you to slow down and be in a state of constant awareness around what you're doing."

She begins a design by researching the function and associated flaws of a particular object so that she can maximize its functionality and simplicity. "Next I start creating a series of prototypes out of paper; once I reach a final design I begin creating the pattern that will be screen printed onto the leather. This is one of my favourite steps in the process as I am able to tap into my artistic side and play around with ways to visually communicate the inspi-

ration behind the product. After the pattern is created I start the technical process of turning the pattern into a screen-printed image. Once printed I begin constructing the bag by marking out and punching each hole and then hand stitching the bag together using waxed linen thread. Finally I smooth and burnish the edges and cover the leather and protective coating and imprint my logo."

By using printed media on the surface of her designs, Angela fuses fine art elements with product design. She cites the Bauhaus school of design as informing her own design principles—that a craft object can fit into the art world and vice versa: "I believe the merging of art with functional designs works to counteract the sometimes austere attitude surrounding art by making it more accessible through the practicality of design. This also elevates the bag to become something more that just an accessory, to an object that can communicate something about the wearer."

Angela's training goes back to her early years when her mother taught her how to use a sewing machine. She later attended Parsons The

New School for Design in New York City with a focus on fashion, but after a year she found that this direct approach to learning about fashion design was not for her. "I enrolled in the Visual Arts program at Emily Carr University in Vancouver, British Columbia. In 2014 I found myself with a BFA in one hand and lump of uncertainty in the other. I felt torn between wanting to return to the practicality of fashion design and also still wanting to evolve my artistic practice. Instead of deciding on one path, I became determined to merge the two fields together; this later became the catalyst for the creation of Epoché."

"Outside my formal education, my creative path has also been greatly influenced by my boyfriend, Kevan D'Agostino, who is a communication designer and also a graduate of Emily Carr University. He has been a huge influence in the way I think about my craft outside of the purely artistic aspects. The knowledge he has given me has been invaluable in helping me to develop and support my craft, through teaching me the importance of design strategy, branding and how to showcase my work. The career highlight of the past year for me was finishing my first collection of products for Epoché and being able to see them side by side in the catalogue my boyfriend helped design."

- **WEBSITE** *epochedesigns.com*
- **BLOG** *epochedesigns.com/blog*
- **SHOP** *epochedesigns.com/collection*
- **TWITTER** *@epochedesigns*
- **INSTAGRAM** *@epochedesigns*

## ON PROMOTING AND SELLING

"Publicly promoting and selling my craft has definitely influenced why and how I go about making new patterns and designs. There is nothing like interacting with your customer to help you understand what they are looking for. When you're creating products just for yourself there's a lot of things you can easily overlook; this changes once you start trying to adapt your designs for others. These interactions have directly influenced my current mission to try to design a backpack that is stylish, practical, light and beautiful."

# HOLLAND SEYDEL

"I think that my hobby for organic gardening pops up in my work in many prominent ways," says artist Holland Seydel from her garage studio in Boulder, Colorado. "Botanical silhouettes reappear through my work and the botanical assemblages are quite recognizable. I also am passionate about being ecological, so many pieces of art feature something old that is given a new life."

Her bohemian parents moved from California in search of a more sustainable lifestyle, so they brought her up in the countryside of Colorado, surrounded by forests, rivers and lakes. "The wilderness for me is a constant source of inspiration. I hated being in the country when I was younger, but now I realize how lucky I was. I am still very outdoor oriented and completely obsessed by nature's botanicals elements."

"I love working with my hands and making ideas materialize; it allows me to express the beauty I see all around me," she explains. "Being very tactile, I must create—there is no other option. It is always enjoyable and leaves me with a feeling of great accomplishment. There is also an element of freedom from restrictions, which appeals to me." In addition to her enjoyment of the surface of things, Holland is passionate about colour. "I may just belong to a colourist sensibility or movement if there is one. The brighter the colours the better. I love fluorescents as well as fleshy coloured worn books. All these colours are directly reflected in nature. Most colours I use come straight from the flower beds."

"I paint mainly oils and work with collage, but enjoy experimenting with many mediums like gouache, watercolour, coloured pencils, cardboard and wood. Most of my works are paintings, some are assemblages. Lately I have been working with floral pieces: petals, leaves, etc. from my garden. They make wonderful

botanical typography. I am also working on a Día de los Muertos (Day of the Dead) sugar skull project in botanical form, which I am photographing to document and preserve it. For the most part I make the art for myself; whomever it appeals to is all for the better."

Depending on the medium she is using she either starts with a sketch or simply starts with the materials at hand. "I've kept sketch books since my architecture school days. But with collage and botanical work I dive right in, paying attention to shapes and compositions. I am super hands-on, slicing and cutting with the help of teeny tiny scissors or X-Actos for precision. For wooden assemblages I sketch my shapes on plywood and then use a jigsaw. No matter which medium, there is always a sizeable mess involved."

Holland appreciates having space to herself

to work and experiment. "I work out of my home in a garage studio, but often I find myself with bits of materials strewn about on the living room floor. I am always finding any available flat surface to create a mess on. However messy it appears, I still seem to know where everything is. It must be some sort of artist savant power."

To offset the isolation of working as a solo artist, she makes sure to get out into the world every day, go for a hike or do some yoga. She is a member of several artist critique groups. "One is for fine art, one for children's book illustration and one for art licensing, which I am just dipping my toe into," she says. "It's crucial to get feedback from other artists who understand the struggle and the drive to create art. Nothing compares to in-person feedback and constructive

criticism. Additionally, I am also part of a few online illustration and writing critique groups." Locally, she has connected with the Boulder chapter of the Society of Children's Book Writers and Illustrators. "I've found amazing friendships, camaraderie and support for perusing, illustrating and writing children's books."

If there is a lull in inspiration, she heads to a flea market to hunt for vintage ephemera and old illustrated books. "There is no comparable feeling to finding a vintage piece that someone else didn't quite appreciate the beauty of. I enjoy changing those things to make them vibrant again." Invigorated by her new direction with florals, she plans on incorporating them into digital collages and move into licensing her work. "I want to incorporate hand-lettered elements into many more pieces and I want to publish my first picture book for children."

- **WEBSITE/SHOP** *hollandseydel.com*
- **BLOG** *hautenature.com*
- **TWITTER** *@hautenature*
- **INSTAGRAM** *@hautenature*

# CHRISTINA ROOS

CALGARY, ALBERTA, CANADA

With her life divided between Calgary, Canada, and Gothenburg, Sweden, Christina Roos calls herself a travelling suitcase artist. But wherever she may be, she always finds a place to work with her art. "As of now, at this moment, I work with pictures and my computer at home in my study in Calgary," she says. "Every six weeks I go to Sweden and work with my ceramics and other things."

Christina is originally from Sweden, and has an MFA in Fine Art and Ceramics from the National Academy of the Arts in Oslo, Norway. She is a mother of two teenagers, aged 17 and 13, and is married to a geophysicist. She also has two dogs: a beagle and a cocker spaniel. "I live as an expat in Calgary, Canada," she says. "I have been moving around in North America; I lived in Texas for nearly six years. My colourful life together with my husband has shaped my creative path. My family in Sweden gives it a touch, too. I travel a lot between Sweden and Canada. I have my studio in Sweden on a small island outside Gothenburg called Öckerö."

"I can't live without doing something creative," says Christina. "It is a restless passion. I have to do things—materialize my thoughts." Working in clay, paper and textiles, as well as some digital work, Christina ardently believes that the things she makes are not only functional, but objects for use in your mind and in your heart. As a studio potter, her cups and mugs are expertly controlled in shape, but adorned with bold graphics. With their organic shapes dripping with colour, her ceramic objects are purposely a bit naïve in their expression. "My things have lot of energy," she says.

"I am lucky to have an interesting life. Travelling gives my soul a lot of inspiration and also the joy with my family."

- **WEBSITE** *christinaroos.com*
- **BLOG** *urbanrabbit-christina.blogspot.ca*
- **INSTAGRAM** *@christinaroos*

# ANNA HRACHOVEC

CHICAGO, ILLINOIS, USA

"I've always been driven to do my own ambitious, weird thing. My style is simple, Japanese-inspired character design in knitted form," says Anna Hrachovec, describing her characters. Referred to as "mochis," they range in size from an inch to several feet tall. "There's a fun minimalism involved in designing them, reducing an animal, person or object to its most essential characteristics. For me, their function is just to exist and be amusing, or perhaps to be a little friend to carry around in your pocket."

"Other people use my designs as toys, as ornaments or as other decor, or even jewellery. The mochis also star in my animations and in the soft sculptures and installations that I make. They tend to be made of wool yarn stuffed with polyester, although sometimes I use styrofoam or foam rubber as a base for larger objects or things that need more structure, like mountains and rainbows."

Anna is part of the new wave of knitting and crochet, and is also part of the kawaii culture that has spread from Japan to the West: "I'm part of the knitting community, which is a broad group but one that gives me lots of inspiration. Much of that community happens on the website Ravelry.com, which is often described as 'Facebook for knitters.' I'm also connected with other character artists around the world through the Berlin-based organization Pictoplasma, who puts on an annual character art festival and other events in various cities."

Originally from Oklahoma, Anna's parents encouraged her to spread her wings. "When I was 17 they sent me off to Japan for a year as an exchange student; it was a challenging and wonderful experience that introduced me to a world of cute and unusual characters that aren't just for children (think Tare Panda and Miyazaki films). This was a big deal for me, since I'd often preferred the company of stuffed animals to kids my age. It was also in Japan that I first learned to knit, from my 28-year-old host sister. (My first project was a purple, fun fur scarf, and I was so proud.) I returned to the US and studied Japanese and film and television

### KNITTING IS MAGICAL

Anna Hrachovec makes things because she finds that there's no feeling more exciting "than to create something that can look back at me. It's magical," she says. "I used to think I would get into making fabric toys once I got tired of knitting, but I've only discovered more and more possibilities with the craft of knitting and new things to do with it (like photography and animation). It's an extremely versatile craft, and the limitations that it does impose are ones that I generally take as a stimulating challenge."

in college, and it was a few years into college that I picked up knitting more seriously. My college boyfriend's mom was a prolific crafter, and we bonded over yarn and needles."

"A few years later, I married my boyfriend and we moved to New York. I got a job at an illustration agency in New York that was headquartered in Tokyo, and within my first year of working there, the agency opened a gallery called hanahou in Soho. To commemorate the gallery's opening, I knitted my first toys, which were blobby monsters made in the shape of the gallery's logo. It was a strange kind of love at first sight when I embroidered eyes onto the blobs and they were looking back at me. At that time, I was feeling super inspired by the illustration and other popular artworks that we handled at the agency and gallery, but I was

also ready for a different job. My husband (who is awesome) encouraged me to take a break and figure out what I really wanted to do, and that's when I started a blog for my knitted toys. Knitters quickly found me online, and the thing that I was going to do between jobs became my new job. My friends at hanahou were supportive of my endeavour and encouraged me to make art with my knitting, and I've found a balance between the craft and art worlds that I love. I call it Mochimochi Land—a realm that encompasses my pattern designing and my art projects, and everything anyone knits from my designs."

Now in Chicago, Anna works out of her home at a desk facing a quiet Chicago street. "I used to do a lot of knitting on the couch, until that started hurting my back. Next to me are big

drawers filled with yarn and stuffing, and nearby is my swift and ball winder. Most of what I do is hand knitting—I use wool yarn, polyester stuffing and a set of double-pointed needles to create my characters and their world. I make terrible sketches to start with, and my designing is a combination of planning and trial and error. Sometimes I get production help from knitting friends, but I have a tendency to just try to knit 30 bunnies in a weekend because I really want to. Occasionally I use a knitting machine to make larger pieces of knit fabric to use as landscape elements like ground and sky."

Though she has had some mainstream success, such as creating knitted animations for the Nickelodeon network, hers is not a typical occupation. "It's challenging to describe what I do for a living to people I meet," she says. "People tend to jump to the conclusion that I just make stuff and list it on an Etsy store all day long (not that there's anything wrong with that!). The most rewarding thing is the feeling that anything is possible—it's all about making, and I can make anything I want. No boss, no rules. (This also probably ties for the most challenging thing.)"

"I don't make selling my knitted characters the focus of my job. I do sell some of my simpler characters on my website, and I also sell my work when I'm part of an art show or doing an installation. In those cases, I think of the sales as secondary to the act of making something new and discovering something different with my craft. Pattern sales, on the other hand, make up a big part of my income—I feel

incredibly lucky that I can knit something once, take photos and write instructions, then sell 100 pdf downloads. The challenge with that is coming up with elegant, easy-to-use designs that other people will want to knit. It's also a challenge to balance my time between coming up with ideas that have mass appeal to knitters and making stuff that pushes my own creativity to new places."

In creating patterns, her customers do the work of replicating and evolving her characters: "It's like I write a piece of code, and then hundreds (sometimes thousands) of knitters execute that code with a seemingly infinite number of variables. I get so many new ideas from them in return—it's a really positive feedback loop. I'm also, frankly, still pretty in love with all of the creatures that I make, and I want to see them multiply and have adventures."

- **WEBSITE** *annahrachovec.com*
- **BLOG** *mochimochiland.com/blog*
- **SHOP** *mochimochiland.com/shop*
- **TWITTER** *@mochimochiland*
- **INSTAGRAM** *@mochimochiworld*

*"There is nothing more satisfying than to make something beautiful that makes people smile."*

ANGELA PRICE

# ANGELA PRICE

VALLEY VILLAGE, CALIFORNIA, USA

"Nature is an amazing artist!" exclaims Angela Price. As a garden designer and maker of tiny terrariums, she is in constant collaboration with Mother Nature. These diminutive gardens are in fact little story worlds, with figurines engaging with the plants in dioramas.

"Each hand-blown glass globe is slightly different, and each scene I create inside them has a unique personality," she says. The figures or artifacts she places within the vessel play with the small scale of the succulents she chooses, accentuating their colours, shapes and textures.

"My terrariums are made from hand-blown borosilicate glass, or Pyrex," Angela explains. "The terrarium starts with a base of succulent soil and mosses. On this prepared 'canvas' I create a scene using miniature model train figures, tiny animals figures, vintage china doll heads, other miniatures, polished stones, pieces of crystal, seashells and other things." Tweezers and chopsticks are her favourite tools for setting the scenes, which range in size from just two to five inches. Angela works closely with a US-based glass blower who custom makes her globes.

When the light is good, Angela takes over her kitchen island to assemble the terrariums. Because she works with dirt, she sometimes prefers to work outside in her yard: "My supplies are stored in a large desk with a hutch.

I am always collecting tiny things and pretty stones, so I have several divided containers to keep things organized. I also have a computer alcove to do my social media and admin work, where I surround myself with little things and quotes that inspire me."

Gardening has been a part of her life since she was a child: "I still remember my family's first vegetable garden, when I was about eight, and the thrill of checking that small plot each morning to see what seedlings had pushed through the soft dirt." Growing up in Los Angeles with an architect father and artist mother, crafting and creating with her mom and gardening with her dad are among her earliest memories. Although she originally trained in the theatre, a career in the entertainment industry was not meant to be. "Life has

a funny way of leading you down a different path," says Angela, "and after struggling as an actor, I found myself working in a human resources office at a high-end retailer. Fast forward a bunch of years—four companies, a husband, two kids and three layoffs—and I was done with the corporate life. I yearned to get back to my creative and artistic roots. While my career has taken me from the theatre to corporate human resources to garden design, I have always been infatuated with gardens."

In the past few years, terrariums and succulent plants have grown in popularity. Angela attributes this to their beauty and ease of care: "I love that my terrarium art is unique but also part of a growing love of indoor gardening."

- **WEBSITE** *edencondensed.com*
- **BLOG** *edencondensed.com/blog*
- **SHOP** *etsy.com/shop/edencondensed*
- **TWITTER** *@edencondensed*
- **INSTAGRAM** *@edencondensed*

GRETTEL CORTES

# ELLEN HOVERKAMP

Ellen Hoverkamp's image-making technique centres around an unorthodox tool: a flatbed scanner. "When I began using flatbed scanners instead of cameras for digital imaging, there were critics who didn't accept the process and product as photography," she says. But acceptance of this photographic niche—sometimes called scenography—is growing, and Ellen's work is an excellent example of its potential.

MARY ANN VOSS

"At exhibitions, I love watching people stop dead in their tracks, stare forward, then come in for a closer look," she says. "Sometimes I'm asked, 'Is it real? Is it a painting or a photo?' followed by questions about technique, and then by praise and their association to the contents of a particular image." Her images are arrangements of garden forms, not only plants and flowers but shells, feathers, nests, eggs, vegetables and more—fascinating in their exploration of depth and composition.

"Because objects are arranged face down on the scanner's glass platen for imaging, it's possible to visually explore a sense of gravity," Ellen explains. "Elements of a composition can appear to be stacked and/or floating. Also, inspired by surface design, I like leading the viewer's gaze throughout multiple focal points within a complex arrangement." This requires

53

creating an arrangement face down on the flatbed scanner, suspending delicate items like peonies with wires from above.

Surprisingly, Ellen describes herself as a novice gardener, with barely a cursory knowledge of plants. "I have found acceptance within a community of knowledgeable gardeners who have supported my artistic efforts over the years. These wonderful people continue to offer their plants and collected natural objects, like nests, eggs and shells, as the subjects for my art," Ellen says. "I scan what other people grow, hoping to bring attention and honour to the efforts of gardeners and to the exquisite beauty of nature."

Instead, she comes from an artistic background: "I was the kid in her room whose moth-

er would continually ask, 'What are you *doing* in there?' I would answer, 'Oh, nothing...' but I would be working on projects. Whether drawing, painting, collaging, knitting, macrame or some other craft, I always was happiest when making things. I still am. I was lucky that my parents didn't consider my creative pursuits a waste of time. In fact, my Mom and Grandmother both drew and painted."

She decided at the age of nine that she wanted to be an art teacher, and followed through on that ambition, teaching art at a public school for 33 years. "Every year of my teaching career was filled with a huge variety of challenges and rewards. Being in the position to influence children to explore and communicate ideas through the mastery of media was a privilege," she says.

Over the years, she developed a broad range of techniques, one after the other: "I approached the pursuit of my own artistic voice like a serial monogamist, intensely learning from relationships with pottery, batik, watercolour, printmaking, video, reprographics and photography, in that order."

She collaborated with the writer Ken Druse on a gardening book titled *Natural Companions*, and is often invited to speak and demonstrate floral scanner photography. She sells prints, notecards and scarves with her work, and has shown her work at both solo and group exhibitions. Her images have also been used on the covers of several magazines.

Ellen creates her work in the basement apartment of her hundred-year-old home. "Garden

flowers may need conditioning, so the sink, bathtub and old, non-defrosting refrigerator come in handy," she says. "I hand-dye silk for the flip sides of my digitally printed scarves and do my sewing in a small room near the kitchen. The main area of my workspace has desks, storage furniture and equipment. Work tables are often littered or decorated (depending on one's view of clutter) with flowers, vegetables, nests, shells, feathers. Unfortunately, our Marty is a bad studio cat who has to be kept upstairs because he eats plants and is too interested in the feathers."

"Making things enables me to feel more fully alive," Ellen says, "providing refuge and connection to a greater community of artists, gardeners and lovers of nature. I strive to create work that serves as a visually powerful, unique reminder that the beauty of nature prevails and that the natural world is worth our care and attention."

- **WEBSITE** *myneighborsgarden.com*
- **BLOG** *myneighborsgarden.blogspot.com*
- **SHOP** *myneighborsgarden.bigcartel.com*
- **TWITTER** *@EllenHoverkamp*
- **INSTAGRAM** *@garden_images*

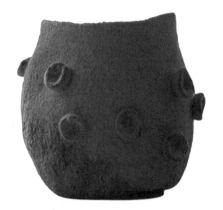

# CHRISTIANNA FERGUSON

### LAKEFIELD, ONTARIO, CANADA

"I actually remember bursting into tears on Christmas morning when I was about 10 years old," recalls felter Christianna Ferguson. "My mother had sewn me a beautiful quilted jacket. I just felt overwhelmed by what I felt to be such an act of love."

Now working out of a bright, sunlit studio space in the woodlands of Ontario, she creates bold, tactile, unique and cozy felt creations. "What is great about it is that it's not in my house, and what is difficult about it is that it is not in my house," she says of the space that she shares with a painter. "I had the space for a full year before my family had even been to see it. I had taken to referring to it as my secret lair."

"Although feltmaking has gained popularity in North America over the last couple of de-cades it is still a craft that many people have not had much exposure to. It is not uncommon for people to examine my work and ask, 'How did you do that?'" Christianna was once one of those people. "I think back 13 years ago when I was first introduced to felting. I had never even heard of it before. Now I look at where feltmakers have taken the medium and it's actually kind of mind blowing. It feels like I am constantly coming across people's work that is so innovative."

Although she spent some time in her twenties travelling in Thailand and India, collecting handiworks that still hang on the walls of her home, her introduction to felting came when she moved with her husband and three kids to Western Australia: "The first day in our new home I picked up the local newspaper and saw an article about some local feltmakers. I spent the next 12 months soaking up the kindness and experience of the women in the Bunbury Felting Group." She has been felting ever since.

Among her varied felt creations are many unique, wearable pieces like scarves, hats and jewellery. "This is the more saleable side of what I do," she says. "I like to think of these items as pieces of art that you can wear that really make a statement. The wearable pieces are made from fine Merino wool and mostly up-cycled silk. They are made for people who value owning something unique and hand-made and aren't afraid to be a little bold."

She's found an unusual place to sell her work: on consignment in the Canadian Canoe Museum in Peterborough, in addition to artisan shows and an open studio tour. "Felting can be a time-consuming process, so having the time to make enough work for sale can be a challenge. I also struggle with pricing. Finding that balance between valuing your work enough to ask for what it is worth but also being realistic about what people may be willing to pay. Over time this has gotten a little easier," she says. She also works on projects that push her technical and artistic skills, including art pieces and hanging textile pieces. "One of my favourite projects was working with a storyteller who was writing a story about a rooster and wanted a rooster puppet he could use to help engage his audience. I'm not a puppet maker so this project provided a creative and technical challenge I would probably not have encountered working in isolation." A polar bear head piece

for a wearable art show was another major recent project.

Through it all, she is still looking to define herself as a creator, still seeing herself in a development stage of her career. "I'm not so sure I have a signature style as of yet, but I strive to create one-of-a-kind pieces that have a big impact," she says. "That being said, I am drawn to simple lines and organic shapes, and often stick to a minimal colour palette, choosing to play with pattern and three-dimensional elements. I really feel that the wool itself is such a beautiful material, I don't like to overwhelm my work with a lot of embellishment."

Classes and workshops were important to Christianna's development, and she gets equal value now out of teaching her craft: "I am always learning new things about the medium when I teach. Learners will also ask you questions that you inevitably won't know the answer to, which requires deeper investigations on your part."

"Making provides such a huge sense of accomplishment," she says. "This is so clear to me when I go into classrooms and felt with children. They are so engrossed in the making process and feel so much pride in the finished product. I believe strongly that creating and making is a human need and contributes to our well being."

- **WEBSITE** *christiannaferguson.com*

# CLEO PAPANIKOLAS

BERKELEY, CALIFORNIA, USA

"Use Cleomade ornaments as gift tags, place cards or save-the-date reminders," Cleo Papanikolas suggests. "Loop them around a bottle or bouquet. Hang them anywhere you would hang a tassel: on chair backs, doorknobs, curtain ties or drawer pulls. Use them as charms for prize ribbons and bookmarks, or as props for play in games of make believe. Dangle them from garlands or tree branches in any season. Or frame them in clusters as art."

Cleo's ornaments straddle the line between greeting tags and works of art: laser-cut decorative objects to which she glues prints of her paintings. "Much of my work has a vintage camp style and some plaid on it somewhere," she says. "I like blending little fine art paintings with crafty woodworking style and modern laser cutting. They seem disparate but go together well."

Her playful motifs include animals, trees, gems and delicacies, and hint at Cleo's roots: "I grew up on a small farm in Northern California. To occupy myself I made mud pies and playthings with supplies gathered from the redwood grove, the creek, the fields and the garage." Later, she spent many years at art school, plus a long career as a professional painter. "I've always been creative, but I worked really hard to become a skilled painter and craftsperson."

She relates her career to the children's book *Harold and the Purple Crayon*, the story of a little boy who draws his adventures: "I've taken

many different career paths holding onto the end of my paintbrush: faux finishes, decorative architectural and furniture painting, mural painting, fine art, illustration for advertising, books and licensing, graphic design and teaching. With such a varied toolbox I'm constantly setting boundaries for myself. Even though I can mix any colour, today I made a piece that was different shades of white."

That toolbox is useful in a process that starts with lists written in a sketchbook, then prototyped with cardboard and drawn as a pencil sketch. She often follows this with gauche and sometimes pen, then moves to a scanner and computer to prepare the laser cutter paths, and finally to glue and scissors to cut out the prints and adhere them to the wood.

Cleo's studio is in her backyard. "I've made it a priority to create my own space," she says. "I try to limit the amount of clutter so I can move about freely and paint large-scale paintings. A clear space also keeps my head clear. But there is always that messy corner full of my kid's projects. My crafting table is covered with a big cutting mat and sheets of newsprint so I can peel off a layer when things get sticky. I have all of my Tiny Paintings Project pieces (a weekly DIY blog craft) pinned to the wall above the table. When I am stuck for a solution and tell myself, 'just do what you know,' I can look up and easily see what I know how to do."

The decision to focus on her own work has been challenging. "To be a painter you have to enjoy spending many hours every day standing in a room by yourself, staring at a wall—and I do: sometimes the wall has really pretty

pictures on it," Cleo says. "But the challenge is to try to make a living doing that. It is a constant cycle of sending queries, sell-sheets, applications and follow-up letters, only to be ignored or rejected. Then reminding myself that it is a game of odds and I'm trying to get a bunch of rejections so then I can get that one good bite. The reward is when someone likes, knows and trusts my work enough to commission something of my own design."

"I made a lot more money when I was working by the hour painting what other people told me to paint. This way, I get to make my own ideas, but everything is on spec. I never know if I'll get paid for my time. It is especially challenging when the added cost of childcare is involved."

But her Cleomade ornaments allow her to sell through craft fairs, online, wholesale and commissions: "I've learned that people usually like to have an excuse to buy things: seasonal gifts, for a good cause, it's a known popular style, as a souvenir, etc. I try to keep a balance between making items that cater to the occasions that people buy things for, and just making random things that I'm inspired to make and then trying to fit them into a sales category. It's important to follow through with the random inspirations in order to progress in art and skill."

- **WEBSITE/BLOG** *cleomade.com*
- **SHOP** *etsy.com/shop/cleomade*
- **TWITTER** *@cleomade*
- **INSTAGRAM** *@cleomade*

# ELYSE WIGEN

"In a world where virtually everything is available to us, people want more and more to be deliberate about the things they choose to consume and to craft their own surroundings," says Elyse Wigen, who makes modern sewn baby goods for her company, Prim Society.

"I think people are drawn to the handmade movement because they can point to a specific person and story behind each item, which adds to the story behind the life they are crafting for themselves, and what they want that story to say about them." This feeling is particularly acute when giving a special gift for a newborn.

Prim Society's signature product is its colour swatch teether toys sets, and it has a personal story as part of its development. "I first came up with the idea of colour swatch baby toys when a close friend from design school was pregnant," Elyse says. "I wanted to give her something unique and personal, and so I thought what if I made a baby version of the

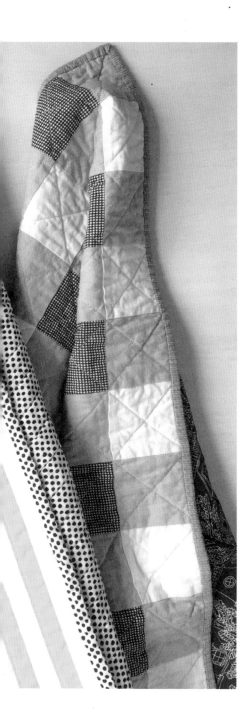

colour swatches she uses every day at her design job?"

"As I made more of these toys as gifts, and as I first started selling them online, I refined the finished product and streamlined the process with each iteration." The Primtone teether sets are available with coordinating bibs, and Elyse also offers beautifully graphic baby quilts and playmats. "My aesthetic is modern, which in my work I define as using basic shapes and bright colours paired with fabric patterns that will coordinate, but won't compete with other objects in the space," she says. "I tend to use techniques from traditional quilt blocks, but mostly make up my own quilt patterns as I go. I try to pair modern designs with the tactile qualities and textures that people love about traditional quilts."

"I'm passionate about design because in many ways it is how we experience the world, be it through good design or bad. My ideas always start from 'a need for' or 'an improvement on'—a way to make something better. It goes back to crafting our lives, which is something that all people share whether we embrace it or not," Elyse explains. "When I look at it in that way, it is hard for me to not be passionate about the talents I have that can make something better for someone else, even in a seemingly insignificant way."

Through interacting with her customers, Elyse has learned that the majority of those purchasing her products are giving them as gifts. With this in mind, she has refined her online shop

and its product presentation so that it is geared towards gifting. She keeps presentation at the back of her mind at every step of creating a product: "How will this look to someone seeing only a photo of it? How would I present it differently to someone who can touch and feel it? What do I want the recipient to experience when they open the box? Asking these kinds of questions has pushed my creativity to ideas I might not have gotten to otherwise."

She has only been working full time on Prim Society for a short while, a transition that happened recently when her husband accepted a job in Memphis: "As we planned our move out of state, I was faced with thinking about what *my* next job would be. I was currently working as a product designer in a corporate setting, running Prim Society on the side, always kind of dreaming about but never fully ready to take the leap into doing my own thing. I decided that this move was my big opportunity to start fresh and do something that was completely my own."

In Memphis, she works out of a corner of their open-plan loft, which was converted from an old cotton warehouse. With three large windows with lots of natural light, tall cabinets full of supplies, a dedicated table for sewing and a desk for computer work, she loves this dedicated space. "It turns out that my creative health is very much tied to light and brightness—which was learned from many years of cramped crafting in badly lit apartments," she says. "Despite all the storage, my workspace is usually overflowing. There's always some

PRIMTON
123 C

PRIMTO
3252 C

PRIMTONE
172 C

"Often times we sell to make a living,
but I think as creatives our ideas can
sometimes be bigger than what is feasible
in terms of equipment or expense.
It's hard to know how much to risk and
what will pay off in the long run."

ELYSE WIGEN

kind of folding table set up to hold the excess, which I always try and convince myself is just temporary," she laughs.

"I'm very motivated by thinking about how lucky I am to get to do what I do. Sometimes it can be hard because a lot of my creative process involves sitting, and thinking, and quietness, which can quickly morph into all-out anti-motivation. But when I imagine going to work at a place where my voice isn't heard as loudly as I think it could be, or where I don't get to make my own creative decisions, or where I can't just drop everything and sew when I feel like it, that pretty much motivates me every time."

Though her business is currently centred around baby products, her vision for Prim Society is more broad: "I want to add home decor and textiles to Prim Society—pillows, large quilts, table linens—as well as stationery and paper products. Somehow it will all work together. The challenge will be adapting my design style to appeal to an adult aesthetic while still keeping the essence of the brand."

At the core of her business is the element of expression through making, of embracing the ability to design one's own surroundings: "My ultimate dream is to design a fabric line so people can do just that—and come up with creations I've never even considered."

- **WEBSITE** *PrimSociety.com*
- **INSTAGRAM** *@elysewigen*

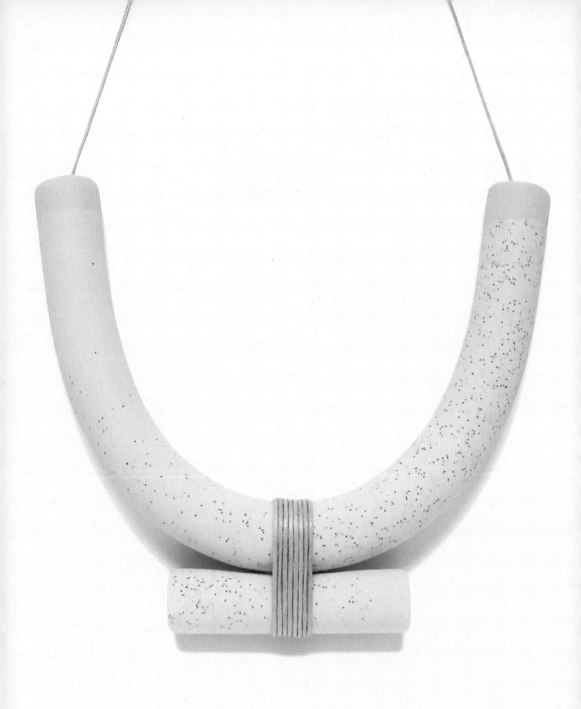

# KATE TROUW

LONDON, UNITED KINGDOM

"In architecture, creative fulfilment can be hard to come by," admits Kate Trouw. "If you are lucky enough to be the lead architect on a project, the actual designing is only about 5 percent of the work you will do and it still takes a huge team and a long time to get anything built. In the end it is other people doing the building; you don't do anything with your own hands during the process."

"Conversely, with making there is a more tangible and instant sense of achievement; it is satisfying to emerge from the spare room after a day of making with an object that is completely my own creation. Therefore, impatience and a selfish desire to be the sole creator have driven my transition from architecture to craft."

Both personal and economic factors also played a role in her migration from architecture to jewellery: "I was working as an architect in London when I was diagnosed with a neurological condition that required surgery. This was around the time of the financial crash,

so once I was ready to go back into employment I found it difficult to find a job, especially one that would allow me the flexibility to deal with my ongoing health problems." She struck out on her own doing freelance architectural work. Around this time, she started attending a pottery workshop. "It had an immediate effect on me. I hadn't realized how much I missed making things by hand and immediately became gripped, to the extent of not being able to sleep at night thinking about all the things I wanted to make."

Class was just once a week, which was too long of an interval for her—not to mention having to wait for pieces to be fired—so she began searching for something similar that she could do at home. "I came across polymer clay," she says. "Of course there are a lot of differences between ceramics and polymer clay, but it was more accessible, and I enjoyed the fact that colour was integral to the material. I started making necklaces for myself, and then as presents for friends, and was encouraged by the response to them so I decided to start a business."

"I hope that the combination of an architectural mindset, a craft practice and a versatile material creates a unique output. I am still refining the style of the work, but elements that feature are 1980s-inflected colour combinations, simple shapes and the incorporation of an element of unpredictability in the process through different colour-mixing techniques." Making jewellery in non-precious materials allows Kate to make statement pieces, but because each is made by hand, the item needs to have a reasonably high price point in order for it to be financially viable. "Some people won't pay above a certain price for a piece of jewellery unless it's gold or silver, and not everyone places a premium on something being handmade rather than mass produced," she says. The good news is that there is demand for her stylish accessories. "Although I have eclectic tastes, I have found, to my surprise, that if I make something that I would love to wear, there are people out there who feel the same."

The polymer clay, also known as FIMO, offers a great variety of experimentation. Her pieces typically have a smooth, matte finish with

pastel colours. The surface is like a delicate eggshell, but the shapes are geometric and simple. "The majority of my designs have arisen through experimenting with the clay and trying out different techniques," she says. "I am fascinated with the ways in which you can mix colours and inclusions, and the stages that the clay goes through before becoming fully mixed. I spend a lot of time at my tiny desk with my pasta machine, rolling and folding the clay, over and over. Once I have created the right mix of clay, I then form it using my hands, knitting needles, sculpting tools and cutters, and bake it in the oven before assembling the final piece."

Though her jewellery enterprise is still less than a year old, she is really taken with the endeavour and its possibilities: "I enjoy the mix of creativity with business and having to be organized, and it is very satisfying to turn an idea into a piece of jewellery a lot faster than a sketch can be turned into a building."

- **WEBSITE** *katetrouw.com*
- **BLOG** *katetrouw.com/blog*
- **SHOP** *katetrouw.com/shop*
- **INSTAGRAM** *@katetrouwjewellery*

# JULIE SINDEN

TORONTO, ONTARIO, CANADA

Julie Sinden makes hats: functional, felted, wool winter hats. She also makes and sells scarves, and spends time on other hand-crafted hobbies, but her hats occupy many corners of her life, from basement to attic, home and abroad.

"My main workspace is in the attic of my home, a warm and sunny space where I spend hours and hours hand stitching," she explains. "I have one large table where I do production, a desk for administrative work and a shipping station. Other parts of my home have also been taken over, most notably the basement, which people are also amazed to see, as it looks like a wool shop. But the great thing about my work is that because so much of it is done by hand, it's very transportable. I spend a lot of time in summer in my hometown, and I take my production with me. My friends and family are very used to me sitting on the hot summer beach, with a pile of wooly hats beside me. My husband is French, and we once spent five months living in France. We had many visitors from Canada, and I would have them bring my hats to work on, and send them back home with the next visitor. That year I thought perhaps I needed to change the label on the hats from 'Made in Canada' to 'Made by a roving Canadian.'"

Julie grew up in a small village on the north shore of Lake Erie, and her family's house was filled with baskets of wool, with a loom in their living room and her mother always with a project in her hands: knitting, spinning, dyeing, sewing, quilting, smocking and felting. Her paternal grandfather was a quilter, embroiderer and woodworker, while her maternal great aunt made images of buildings that were important to her. Unfortunately, Julie spent many of her early years in and out of the hospital, and cross-stitching, needlepointing and knitting all provided comfort during that time. She drew a design for her first sweater (later knit by her mother) when she was 10. Eventually she decided she wanted to make a living creating things, and attended the Kootenay School of the Arts in British Columbia, majoring in textiles.

Julie sees a niche in making wool hats: "In cold climates, having the proper clothing to keep you warm is essential, but much of the time, this clothing forces you to sacrifice style. The two comments that I most frequently get from my customers is that the hat is the warmest they have ever owned, and that they get so many compliments when they wear it. It's the best of both worlds. My signature style is a vintage/modern look. The hats feel like they are from a different era, without being costumey." She has sold hats to young kids and much older women, with most of her customers being in their 30s and 40s. "One of my favourite memories from the One of a Kind Show was selling

the same hat to a sweet teenage girl and her 80-year-old grandmother," says Julie.

She sells her products on Etsy and at events like the One of a Kind Show, which gives her the chance to connect directly with customers, many of whom are passionate about buying handmade and local.

Like so many makers, Julie has had to balance what she can make a living from and what she is most passionate about. "Some processes are just so labour intensive that it's not realistic to sell them," she says. "For example, I am very passionate about dyeing with natural dyes, and much of my work at school focused in this area. I still love to dye, but it is a very difficult type of work to do if you're trying to make a living from it—it's just so time consuming, and the price of the finished product would be astronomical. So it's necessary to find that balance, especially if you hope to make your living from your craft alone. You need to find something that you like to make, but that also lends itself to production making."

Julie has found a silver lining in this: "I'm also happy that I don't do the dyeing as my main source of income, because that can be another challenge when you are selling creativity. It's important to keep some things for yourself, as passions. And I am very fortunate that I get to teach dye classes, as I still get to share my love of natural dyeing. And in a way that is so satisfying, as I then get to see the wonderful things that people make with the skills I have shared with them."

"You have to wear many different hats," she says about her work. In addition to design, there's marketing, bookkeeping, shipping and ordering, managing employees and inventory. She is also a mother to a one year old, which means she is learning to juggle work and family in a whole new way.

Because she exclusively makes winter hats, she also finds benefit in the seasonal nature of her work: "I am fortunate that at different times of the year I am focused on different tasks, which means that I am able to step back from the work and come back to it rejuvenated. In late winter and early spring I take some time to experiment and play, making things strictly for fun. Right now I am working on a quilt, a knitted bunny and dresses for myself and my daughter. Although these projects could be placed more in the category of hobby, they invariably end up influencing my actual work when I go back to it," she says.

- **WEBSITE** *juliesinden.com*
- **SHOP** *juliesinden.etsy.com*
- **INSTAGRAM** *@julieschmulie*

MODEL SHOTS BY CELINE KIM

### DOING THE WORK OF CENTURIES, STITCH BY STITCH

Julie believes that she is a maker because it's in her blood. "It is something I have always been doing. I have also always been interested in how things are made, and in who makes them. I am also a born traveller and my favourite journeys have been to places with rich textile histories, such as Japan, Guatemala and Morocco. I feel honoured to be doing work that has been done for centuries, all over the world, and to continue a tradition of making things by hand, stitch by stitch."

"There is a strong desire for many people these days to know the story behind the things they are buying and to purchase work that they know was made by people who have been fairly compensated and enjoy what they do. Because this often means that the cost of such items is higher than mass-produced work, it's necessary to shy away from the more immediate trends of fast fashion."

# CHANDLER O'LEARY

TACOMA, WASHINGTON, USA

Chandler O'Leary grew up in a military family, and her nomadic childhood influences her to this day. "Moving to a new place every few years gave me a lifelong love of both travel and learning—as well as a strong sense of place in my work," she says. "It also instilled a need to document life as I move through it. I started keeping sketchbooks as a teenager, as a way to record and remember my experiences through drawing."

Chandler lived in Rome during her junior year at the Rhode Island School of Design, where she kept sketchbooks with colourful drawings that filled up the pages from edge to edge. "My sketchbooks have followed the same format ever since. These days, drawing from direct observation has become an integral part of every aspect of my work—from client projects to stationery designs to the sketchbooks I still fill on a daily basis."

An illustrator and lettering artist, Chandler also has a background in letterpress and book arts: "When I first started my business, Anagram Press, I was mostly letterpress printing and hand binding my work in limited editions; these days I am shifting my focus more toward painted pieces and digital reproduction." Self-directed work is an integral part of Chandler's practice. "Aside from my studio work, I

lighting places and attractions around North America," she explains. "The blog has garnered a large, international following since I started it in 2013. It has also led me to several travel-themed studio projects, including my in-progress 50 States series."

A professional creative for many years, she has seen trends come and ago. "I have a history of getting interested in things that are deeply out of favour at the time, and that only later begin to become popular," she says. "I got into letterpress printing a couple of years before it started becoming popular, and have been both lettering and keeping sketchbooks for over 20 years, while for most of that time the larger art world was either unaware or uninterested in it." She officially started her business in 2004, when hand lettering wasn't *de rigueur*. "I constantly had to field the 'what font is that?' question, and explain what lettering is. And for many years, when I was out drawing in my sketchbook, people would ask me if I was a student—you just didn't see people out sketching in public otherwise. In the past few years, though, the pendulum has swung back around to both lettering and sketchbook drawing, and all of a sudden I'm part of something that's popular. That has been both a blessing and a curse. I love seeing my work more readily accepted now that it's 'on trend,' but it can be frustrating to be accused of being trendy when you've been doing that type of work for years and years."

am known for my work on two different side projects, both of which influence and drive my other illustration work. The first side project is a collaborative letterpress broadside series called the 'Dead Feminists,' which I create with fellow artist Jessica Spring. For that series, I am the illustrator and letterer, and Jessica is the letterpress printer. With that series, Jessica and I take quotes from women in history and tie them into current political and social issues. Each broadside is hand lettered in a historical style that matches the era in which each feminist lived, and is illustrated with imagery that ties into the issue at hand."

Her other side project is the blog Drawn the Road Again, which combines her love of travel with sketching. "Drawn the Road Again is thematic rather than chronological, high-

Whether drawing an historical figure or documenting a place, Chandler considers drawing

My CIRCUMSTANCES compel me to Become MASTER of MY OWN BOAT

ELIZA ★ THORROLD ★

1860 ~ 1935

Ethel & Marion

an extension of learning. "When I draw something," she explains, "I'm studying it intensely, and focusing all my attention on understanding the anatomy of something, or the way something works, or the complex perspective of a viewpoint. I am interested in absolutely everything, and incorporating what I see into my work is my way of learning more about the world around me. People frequently tell me they've learned something new from my art pieces—but it's the same for me, as well. By drawing what I see and researching each piece,

I'm learning things I never would have discovered as a student. That's really what drives my passion, and I hope I never lose that."

Like many artists, she is also a collector, but she tries to keep the urge to amass in check. "I try not to accumulate too much stuff in my life, yet I'm intensely attracted to objects and ephemera," she says. "My travel sketchbooks satisfy much of that urge to collect things, because they collect and house my memories from each trip. Each is a finished work of art in and of itself, a book that tells the story of

a journey from beginning to end. When I go back through each sketchbook, I remember details from the trip that photographs could never trigger, all because I took the time to really sit and study my surroundings. Because of that, my sketchbooks are the best travel souvenirs I could ever ask for—and they make me yearn to capture whatever the next adventure might be."

Chandler has put down roots in Tacoma, Washington: "Tacoma is a both an art-friendly place and a community that understands that the arts are a viable economic engine. There are many, many artist-entrepreneurs here, and there are a lot of programs to support working artists—individual artist grants, a huge public art program, studio coops, a city-subsidized program to pair artists and arts businesses with empty storefront spaces, awards for arts innovators, a city-wide arts month and annual studio tour circuit, etc. As a result there is a

huge (and growing) creative community here, a supportive network of artist-owned small businesses and seemingly endless opportunities for both emerging and established artists." There is a community of letterpress printers and book artists, and Chandler participates in many related events.

"My husband and I bought a historic Craftsman house six months ago, so I'm settling into a new studio space," she says. "My studio actually consists of several spaces in my house: a dedicated workroom, an annex that holds my flat files and supplies, inventory storage for my stationery upstairs and a small space in our finished basement for my printing and other equipment. My main studio is my workroom, though—it's a room that was added onto the house in 1936. Our house is built on a hill, so my studio is cantilevered over the back yard. The room is small (about 100 square feet), but it doesn't feel cramped, as it has a balcony ac-

cessed by French doors, and huge corner windows with a view of Puget Sound and Maury Island. The space is dominated by an eight-foot Douglas fir work table under the picture window and bookshelves crammed with art history and design books. It's also the only room in the house where I deviated from traditional Craftsman decor, and allowed myself to go crazy with colour. I love surrounding myself with warm, vibrant hues (maybe it was all those years of rentals and military housing, where I was never allowed to paint the walls!), so my studio is full of brightly coloured folk art and vintage fruit crate labels, hung on robin-egg-blue walls. My space is still a work in progress, but I love that for the first time in my life, it's my very own."

- WEBSITE/SHOP *chandleroleary.com*
- BLOG *drawntheroadagain.com*
- TWITTER *@anagrampress*
- INSTAGRAM *@drawntheroad*

## MIXING IT UP

"I've been selling my work for over 11 years: online (Etsy, Scoutmob and my own web shops), wholesale at brick-and-mortar shops, through galleries and dealers, and at live events like craft fairs and artisan markets. I also take client commissions, although I prefer selling and licensing my existing work, as all of those pieces are self-directed. My income is really a mix of all of these things (client work, fine art, licensing, my own products, grants, etc.), and I rely on having a lot of eggs in a lot of baskets to make my living."

"That mix of income streams is both exciting and difficult—it takes a lot of plate spinning to make those things work. Running a retail/wholesale business (including live events) takes a lot of time and energy away from creating new work in the studio. I love having dealers and galleries sell some of my work, but I've found that that model is not nearly as common as it used to be. Gone are the days (if they ever really existed in the first place) where the artist's only job was to make new work, and it was somebody else's job to sell it. That means artists need to be entrepreneurs as well, and that's a tough juggling act. At the same time, nobody can tell the story of my work better than I can, and I've found that customers and audiences really appreciate getting to know the artist behind the work. So wearing all the hats is an important part of being an artist today, and can be as rewarding as it is challenging."

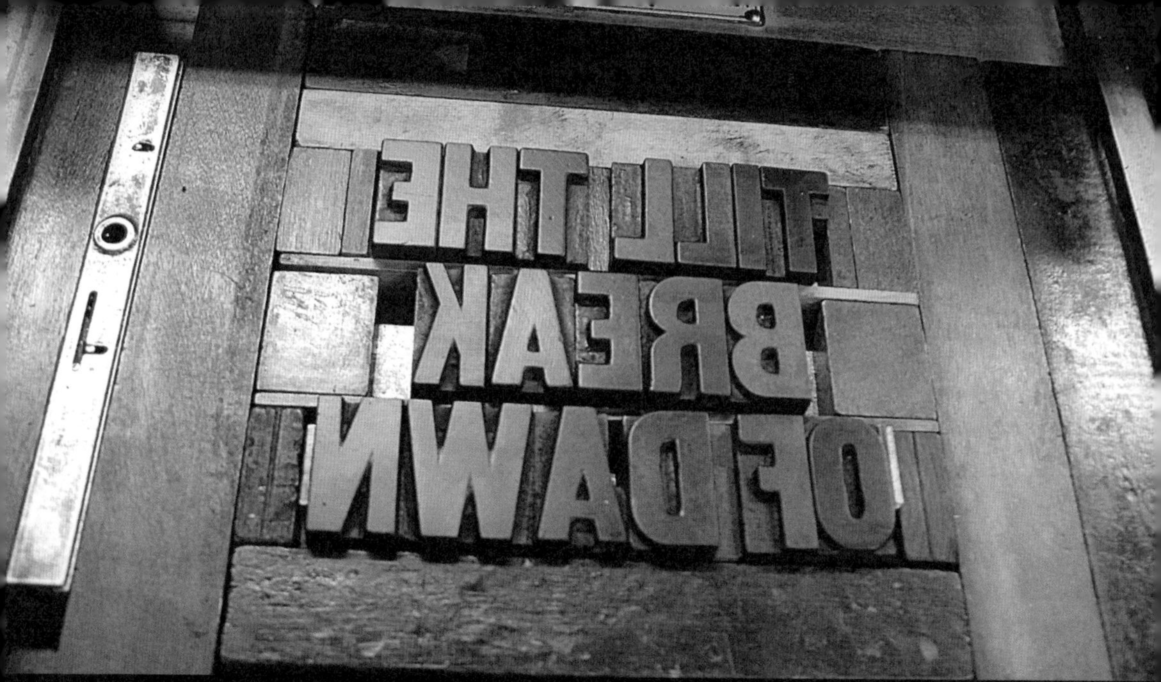

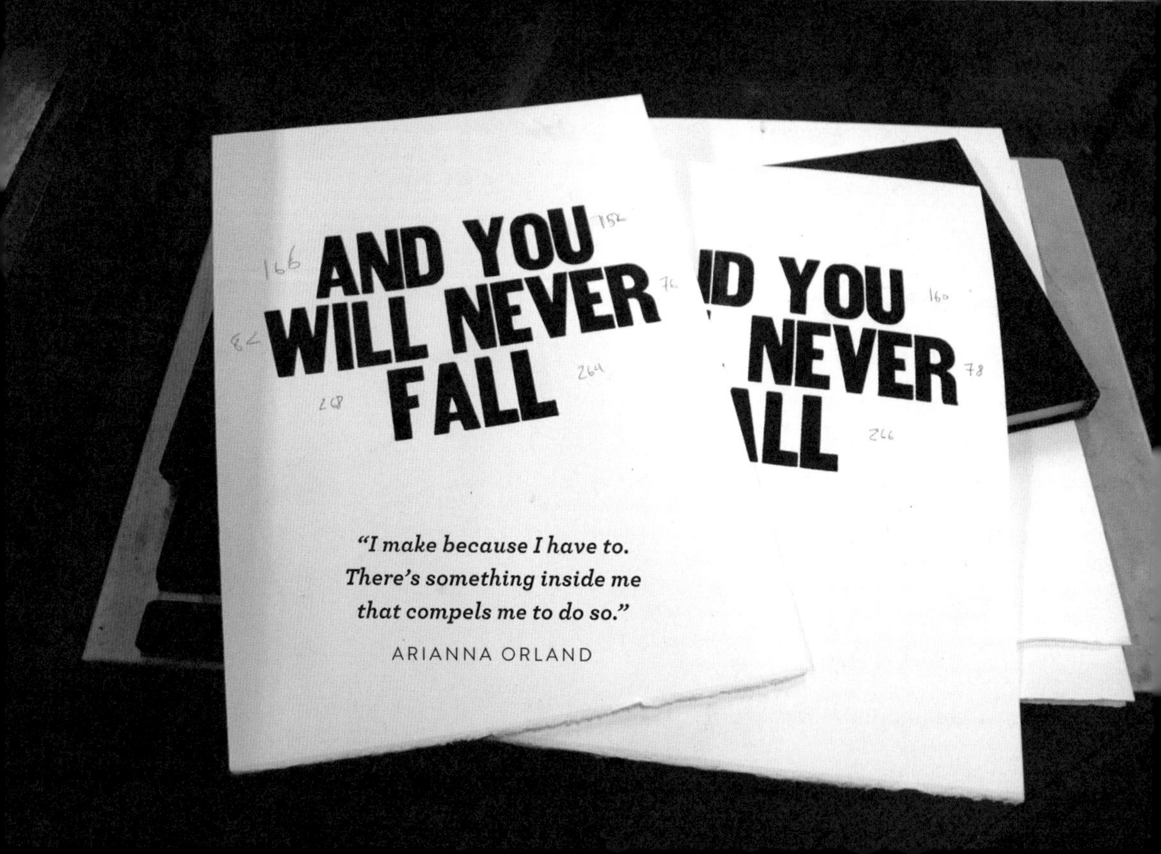

TILT THE BREAK OF DAWN

AND YOU WILL NEVER FALL

*"I make because I have to. There's something inside me that compels me to do so."*

ARIANNA ORLAND

# ARIANNA ORLAND

SAN FRANCISCO,
CALIFORNIA, USA

Arianna Orland is a designer, teacher, artist and maker who grew up in Southern California on healthy doses of sunshine and frozen yogurt.

"I've been fortunate enough to have more than a few shepherds along my creative path," she acknowledges. "The first would be my dad because he gave me access to tools and technology as a child and is a writer himself. He views art with reverence and taught me that being an artist is a vocation to be respected. Next is my mom who gave me boundless encouragement and reassurance in my abilities. My college thesis advisor John Dizikies is also on the list. He invited me into a discourse on art history and aesthetics and always treated my ideas with merit. And finally, I'd like to include Hillman Curtis, the late new media designer and filmmaker. He was a dear friend and mentor who showed me that my creative voice has meaning and can inspire others."

Arianna makes typographic letterpress posters using turn-of-the-century wood type:

## AND YOU DON'T STOP

"The minimalist affirmations are daily reminders to have courage and optimism, and in equal parts." Her most well-known poster has the statement "Everyday I'm Hustlin" letterpressed in a bold sans serif. It was widely popular on the Internet, and is also offered as a temporary tattoo through Tattly, a business card with MOO and wall graphic with Blik. She also sells it through her own Paper Jam Press.

Arianna first learned how to letterpress at the San Francisco Center for the Book, and she returns often to print new work: "My dad got me an intro to letterpress printing class there. In most intro classes they tell the students to pick a phrase to print so they can learn to set the type and operate the machines. It turns out picking a phrase causes some anxiety for people. Teachers know this and offer books or even fortune cookies to help people along. The first phrase I printed was to someone I love. I was living in the Mission District of San Francisco at the time and there was an artist who spray painted phrases on the sidewalk. It seemed they were in love, too, and maybe

things weren't going so well. I took a picture of 'Love me till my heart stops,' from the Talking Heads song 'This Must Be the Place,' and kept it on my desk. When it was my turn, that's the phrase I printed. It was then I realized how powerful a few well-chosen words could be."

Her posters are simple and start with Gothic wood type printed in black ink on cotton rag paper. "That's it. I don't deviate from the style and that's intentional. For me, making them is a meditation on graphic design process and form. But there's something else going on, too, once the ink hits the paper and that headline type does what it was designed to do, the posters command your attention and they make you think. As for the phrases, I choose them carefully to elicit confidence and maybe even a smile. I figure everyone can use a reminder or a push from time to time, and if you happen to recognize the songs the posters reference, even better."

The work is very much a writing and editorial process, so she jots down phrases as they come to mind. When she is ready to do a new edition, she goes over the long list with a second opinion. "My boyfriend and I debate the merits of each phrase until there's a list of between 8 to 12 posters," she explains. "I do the printing at San Francisco Center for the Book where they have several beautiful presses that you can rent by the hour if you have a certain amount of proficiency on a press. The machine I like is called Beluga, a Vandercook proof press probably from the 1970s. The Center also has a large collection of type cases, furniture, pica rulers and everything else you need to run a print shop. Since the Center is a communal workspace there are often other letterpress printers using the facility at the same time."

The finished posters are brought to a home office dedicated to Paper Jam Press projects. "I have a production table used for framing and packaging up orders. I keep some of the poster inventory here and some of it I store with my drop shipper. I just moved in to this office a couple months ago and it's the first time I've had a dedicated space for the business."

Inspirational mantras and graphical sayings have been part of a noticeable trend, something that Arianna accepts: "I don't know that my work is unique but I do think it's gotten to be somewhat recognizable. While it's true I might be one of a handful of people that letterpress prints hip-hop phrases, I'm definitely not the only person who prints posters they think people will care about. I have been doing it for over five years now and the work has been shared and talked about quite a bit online. Sometimes it gets attributed to me and sometimes it doesn't. I'm ok with that. Of course I like getting credit but I don't do it solely for that reason. I make the posters because it makes me happy; looking at them on my walls makes me happy. It's extremely gratifying to offer them up to other people and see where they end up."

She knows the effort that goes into her prints, having acquired the expertise through practice and patience. "The work requires me to touch

JULIA ROBBS

things, to measure and to use my hands," she says. "I have to put physical effort into the work in order to see it manifested in the world. It's the opposite of digital expression in that way. There's an imperfection to the process that forces me to navigate the quirks inherent in a manual process. The craft is both technical and human. Going through the process of cranking out each print one at a time connects me to a sense of responsibility for the individual objects I create. The posters that result from this process are both fragile and definitive at the same time."

- **WEBSITE/SHOP/BLOG** *paperjampress.com*
- **TWITTER** *@paperjampress*
- **INSTAGRAM** *@paperjampress*

## ON SELLING YOUR WORK

"I think there are a couple challenges with selling craft and creativity. One is on the business side of things and deciding where to spend your time. So much of selling craft has nothing to do with being an artist or a maker and everything to do with things like business acumen and social marketing skills. I struggle most with figuring out what can be delegated and finding support. The second challenge is in communicating the value around craft. Some people see craft as something they could do if they just had the time. This is particularly true with my work where the letterpress aspect goes unnoticed and people think, why should I pay for something I can make in Microsoft Word and print out myself. The fact is they can, but they don't. I think the act of making is an act of bravery where we as artists consciously decide to bring objects into being for others to enjoy or to help them experience the world in a new way, and that's just magic."

IT WAS ALL A DREAM

99

# COURTNEY MURPHY

MISSOULA, MONTANA, USA

For years, Courtney Murphy was a bit of a ceramics nomad, travelling around the US attending different residencies. In 2009 she moved to Montana for a residency in Helena. Then another in Red Lodge, Montana. Then in Missoula, Montana. She took the plunge and bought a house in Missoula, and is now part of that state's formidable clay community.

"People often make long drives to attend openings or workshops in different cities around the state," Courtney says, "so there's a great deal of support and sharing of information within the clay community here. I feel lucky to be a part of it." The studio she now shares is in downtown Missoula, five blocks from her house. "It's in a very old building, with a patchwork of linoleum and wood floors. It used to be a bar about 30 years ago. My area is longer than it is wide, with a wheel, some crowded shelves and a wooden work table that a friend built, where I do all of

my decorating. Over the table I have a collection of posters, postcards and other inspiration on the wall. It is never as clean as I wish it was. My favourite part is a big, full-length window to the left of my table. The late-afternoon light makes everything look beautiful."

There, she creates ceramic work—often mugs and nesting bowls—which she describes as unique in its simplicity of form and subtle use of line and pattern. "It functions to add some beauty to everyday routines like morning coffee or dining with friends. It's made for someone who appreciates good design and thoughtfully made handmade objects."

Because she works in multiples, her ideal studio process is an effort in multitasking. "When I'm in a good studio rhythm, I like to have things going in different stages," she explains. "Ideally as the mugs I threw are drying, the plates are ready to be trimmed, and when that's done, the mugs are ready for handles to be made and attached. My most satisfying studio days are the days when the temperature and airflow are just right, things are drying at a good rate, and I can move from one stage to the next fairly seamlessly and get a lot accomplished in the day."

Courtney sees handmade ceramics as part of a larger trend: "There is a trend of greater appreciation and interest in thoughtfully handmade objects, both in crafts as well as in the local food movement. The two things seem to complement each other. As people are spending more time preparing their food and thinking

about where their food comes from, I think it makes sense to want to eat and serve thoughtfully made food off of thoughtfully made dishes, and know that your dishes were made by an actual person."

When she was growing up, trips to museums with her parents fuelled her creativity, as well as watering houseplants for her globe-trotting neighbours, whose home was a museum in itself: it was, as she describes it, "a little stone house that was filled with tapestries, puppets, ceramics, carved wood panels and other objects from their travels all over the world. I loved being in their house and spending time with all of these objects." However, it was not until after college that she took her first ceramics course. "Even though I was terrible at it in the beginning, it just consumed my thoughts. I was never bored in the studio, and always curious to learn new things." More classes followed, as well as a work-trade exchange with a potter, which opened her up to the possibility of making a career out of ceramics.

That career is always a work in progress. Her greatest challenge? "Figuring out how to make a living, and getting used to the ebbs and flows of work and income. Usually the months leading up to the holidays are really busy, and also good sales-wise. Afterwards, things slow down a lot, and it can be hard to keep the same levels of motivation, when the demand has lessened."

She also struggles with promoting her work. Primarily she has sold her work through ceramics galleries, though she gets more satisfaction from direct sales, and not only because of the cut that galleries take. "I really enjoy direct sales, and the opportunity to see and hear what people are responding to," she says. "Sometimes I'll be really excited about a piece with a new design or a new pattern, and people just don't seem that interested. Meanwhile, another piece that I wasn't particularly excited about seems to get a lot of attention."

Looking forward, she intends to branch out into the design world more. She admits that the business side of things is a weak spot for her, but she has made it a goal to focus on that, as well as to explore new challenges in her own work: "Because my forms are relatively straightforward, I'd like to start slip casting some of the pieces—saving time in the actual making of the piece so that I have more time to experiment with new and different surface decorations."

"I'm not sure I ever made a conscious decision to be a maker," Courtney says. "I just know that when I found ceramics, I found something that captured my interest on a more intensive level than anything else I had ever done. It's something you could spend a lifetime doing and never learn it all, or feel bored by it."

- **WEBSITE/BLOG** *courtneymurphy.net*
- **STORE** *courtneymurphy.net/mugs*
- **INSTAGRAM** *@courtneymurphyceramics*

# DEBBIE KENDALL

PENN, BUCKINGHAMSHIRE, UNITED KINGDOM

"I was totally blindsided and unprepared for the amazing bond that I would have with my dog, a Portuguese Water Dog called Figo," relates Debbie Kendall, proprietor of The Enlightened Hound. "He is my first dog and he is always there for me—loyal, funny, uplifting, incredibly calming—and it's very difficult to be anything but happy in his company. The unshakeable bond between humans and dogs is timeless and will always be the inspiration behind my work," Debbie explains. "My prints are a celebration of that bond and a reminder of the joys of sharing our lives with these amazing animals."

With hand-drawn letters and a nod to old-fashioned ephemera, her style is deliberately idiosyncratic and wonky, as she characterizes it: "I often combine it with illustration and vintage decorative elements typical of 19th century ephemera. Sometimes I print over actual ephemera items, like old medicine bottle labels. I love the quirks and colloquialisms of the English language, with its curious idioms and turns of phrase, and enjoy finding ways that these can be incorporated into my prints."

The process for creating a linocut is arduous. "New prints usually start life as a series of pencil thumbnail sketches, doodles and lettering ideas," Debbie explains. "Once the visual layout is confirmed I need to consider the technical printmaking implications of achieving the

final print. Printmaking requires an ability to think in layers of colour, as each colour generally needs a separate printing plate. Colours, or plates, are printed one at a time, and the prints are hung up to dry in between colours."

The relevant parts of a design are separated into each colour and transferred onto a piece of linoleum: "Then I can begin to cut out the design. Letters have to be carved in reverse, so that they are the right way round when they are printed. I do this using woodcarvers gouges. They have very sharp steel edges and rounded wooden 'mushroom' handles that fit beautifully in the palm of my hand. Cutting the lino is painstaking, intense and therapeutic. Each cut is final—there is little room for error. It can take up to a week to carve a plate, depending on its complexity."

The process continues: "Once the plates are ready I can start to print. I roll out the colour onto the lino plate and then lay down the paper on top. To transfer the ink onto the paper I pass the paper and plate though my etching press. I use traditional oil-based printing inks. They have very intense colours and are thick and sticky and they take a while to dry, so I can only print one colour every couple of days. I mix up my colours by hand and therefore colours between batches of prints vary slightly. I use strips of paper as 'recipe cards' for the colours I have mixed so I remember how to recreate them next time."

Her studio is a converted attic ("With the most amazing views over the treetops!") Debbie has even made some of the furniture herself, such as a series of stacking cubes made from thick plywood and acrylic to hold her many books. "I also have an old 1920s wooden plan chest with brass cup handles and label holders to store papers and prints," she says. "My homemade print drying rack takes up the length of one wall and can hold over 100 prints. I also have to make room for framing tools and materials

and packaging supplies like bubble wrap and corrugated card. The floor is cork, which is soft and warm underfoot, clean and a great ready-made cutting surface for craft projects! And of course, there is a dog bed for Figo."

"I love the physicality of printmaking," says Debbie. "The sticky, messy inks, the sharp gouges for linocutting, the hiss of the brayer as it rolls out the ink, the mechanical clanking of the press and the thrill of pulling the paper from the inked plate to reveal the image." With the duality of creativity and technical ability, Debbie knows that printmaking is the perfect medium for her: "I am curious about how things are constructed, so the mechanical and technical elements of creating a print appeal to my practical side, whilst getting the illustrative and graphic composition of the image right satisfies my artistic side. I like nothing better than solving a creative brief, whether it be from a client or self imposed. I worry that there will never be enough time to learn everything I want to know about printmaking, but every day I learn something new from practice and experimentation and just 'doing'."

"I am happy and proud to be a 'maker,'" says Debbie. "People have always appreciated individual, handmade items that reflect the craftsmanship and expertise of their maker. However, I think this is even more true today because of the fast pace of life in the Western world and the economic pressure to produce goods as quickly and cheaply as possible. Nowadays, handmade items stand for more than originality, individuality and artistry, but also a cherishing of tradition and a valuing of people as masters of their trade—the antithesis of mass production."

- **WEBSITE** *theenlightenedhound.com*
- **BLOG** *inkydogpress.wordpress.com*
- **TWITTER** *@HoundArtPrints*
- **INSTAGRAM** *@theenlightenedhound*

# DORIT ELISHA

Dorit Elisha grew up in Israel with her father, a professional photographer, and her mother, a very crafty person. But her grandmother—a thrifty woman who recycled everything she could—also contributed to Dorit's creative growth.

"Usually for me the inspiration comes from the materials that I find," Dorit says. "I scavenge flea markets and thrift stores, find something intriguing—such as an old book, an old map, an old piece of embroidery—and go from there. I decide whether it will be a two- or a three-dimensional object, then find the additional components it needs. Sometimes it may take a few hours, sometimes days or weeks."

It is a process that takes over her entire house: "I take over every table, shelf and chair, and clear them only when we have company. The reason is that in addition to being an art teacher in my day job, I also work on several projects at the same time. So my students' artwork and mine need a lot of space! In addition to that, like many artists I have accumulated a lot of materials and supplies for my art and these are piled everywhere as well."

This approach permeates not only her art but her work as a teacher as well. She is a member of RAFT (Resource Area For Teaching), an organization that provides teachers with recycled materials for the classroom.

The result of this process is work that is rich with texture and colour, and deeply personal. "My art is made mostly for myself, because I feel that I have to," says Dorit. "Its function is to make me feel accomplished, happy, calm. Often it is a decorative piece that adds colour to my home. I move from one medium to another constantly, and from one style to another—sometimes vintage, sometimes colourful printed patterns—but the common qualities are always colour and texture."

Although Dorit does occasionally sell her work, usually at local craft fairs, she always finds it a challenge to let go of something she has invested herself in: "Selling my artwork to someone who appreciates it is a wonderful feeling, but I will not change anything that I do in order to sell more. I create for my own pleasure before anyone else's. I just know that I have an inner need to create, to make stuff, to see and to create beauty; it makes me feel great, happy, satisfied. I knew that from a very young age."

She is a member of the Bay Area Book Artists, and creating artist books is a great opportunity for her to stretch her creative skills. "My artist books, for example, have printmaking, stitching, fiber, collage—all mixed together. I am also known to follow the notion that more is more. I am definitely not a minimalist!"

Her work afforded her the opportunity to be an artist in residence at the International School of Design in Venice, Italy. In 2009 she published a book about mixed-media techniques, and looks forward to publishing more in the future.

- **WEBSITE** *doritelisha.com*
- **BLOG** *lifeasafiveringcircus.blogspot.com*
- **SHOP** *goodgoods.etsy.com*

# DINARA MIRTALIPOVA

Dinara Mirtalipova was born and raised in Tashkent, Uzbekistan, where local art and craft had a major influence on her. "I soaked up my native culture and folklore through my grandmas," she says. "But I never believed art could be a real profession and I always considered it as just my hobby."

Instead, she went to a school of economics and studied computer science and cybernetics. Shortly after she graduated, however, her family moved to the US and she found herself working at American Greetings, where she discovered an amazing world of illustration: "Since that day I was never the same person. I spent a good eight years working shoulder to shoulder with amazing artists and designers, learning from them and practising on my own."

Then in 2014 she left that comfortable position to start her own textile design company, while continuing to freelance. Her business, Mirdinara Kitchen, makes tea towels, and she is working hard on adding additional products—tablecloths, placemats and napkins—to her offerings. She is even considering making porcelain dishes.

"I'm forever a learner/student," says Dinara. "I like signing up for classes and workshops, like printmaking, woodcarving, dish making, clay

throwing, etc. It is always unpredictable where my object/craft can get it's life from."

Her textiles, made of heavy cotton, are beautifully packaged and ready to be given as a gift. Every towel comes with a recipe card wrapped inside. "I like my textiles to be bold, bright and happy," she says. "I noticed they tickle nostalgia in people. I guess they all reflect my taste for folklore, as it shows in the colour combination I'm playing with and design elements I'm choosing. I like drawing animals and birds decorated with lots of florals."

She sells her towels through her own website as well as on Etsy, and balancing her creative ambitions with making a retail product can be challenging: "I've learned how to be more flexible. For example, the price people are comfortable with paying for your product dictates what you can and cannot do with your product. I had this crazy idea of a super decorated packaging box for my towels, but it was very costly and I would never put my customers in that situation where they had to overpay. So I had to opt out and quickly come up with an alternative solution, while still making the packing looking festive."

Although she attends events like Surtex and sells her towels at Renegade Craft Fairs and other events, she considers herself an introvert: "I'm more comfortable working in peace and quiet."

"I used to have a clean nice desk dedicated to working and painting," she recalls. "But then I became a parent, and right now I can say my workspace is *everywhere*! It's been an amaz-

*"The word 'trend' scares me. 'Trend' means massive obsession over something particular and specific—it could be a certain colour or subject matter. I shut myself out from following what is trendy as I have found my inner voice, and I will protect that vision and reserve it for people who like my style for what it is, and not because something is popular this year."*

DINARA MIRTALIPOVA

ing three-and-a-half years since I had Sabrina. Since the time she was born I realized that my quiet days are forever gone and if I wanted to stay being creative I would just have to adjust my attitude to my process. So we have many portable containers of paints and brushes around the house. Now Sabrina is a curious child and she has become my partner in crime; we paint while eating our breakfast, on a plane, in a park, in pajamas, in the kitchen, in the living room—everywhere and everytime. I'm going to rent a real studio soon where we won't worry so much about ruining the carpet."

But despite the energy of the day, some of her best work happens at night. "Every night, after everybody is asleep and it gets quiet in the house, I like painting and sketching," she says. "Usually the majority of my motifs come through that process. Some little paintings

may become patterns and others may be developed further for a conversational piece."

"Sometimes I can't even fall asleep because all the ideas are floating around. There are so many things I could do if only I had more hours in a day and more arms. Movies, poetry, books, music—it all influences me. But maybe the biggest of all of them is my nostalgia for my grandma's living room. I guess I'm trying so hard to reincarnate that through my art, and honestly I don't know if that goal is ever reachable."

- WEBSITE *mirdinara.com*
- BLOG *mirdinara.blogspot.com*
- SHOP *mirdinarakitchen.com/shop*
- TWITTER *@mirdinara*
- INSTAGRAM *@mirdinara*

# HEATHER REINHARDT

CALGARY, ALBERTA, CANADA

"I make T-shirts!" says Heather Reinhardt enthusiastically about her company, Mumble Tease. "Well, I began with just T-shirts, but now I print on many other wearable things like sweaters and scarves, and I make things like printed wall hangings from fabric, tote bags and cards—but mostly T-shirts. T-shirts have been a great way for me to share my art and my unique sense of humour with a wide audience. I like to think I'm brightening the world one shirt at a time."

A graduate from the Alberta College of Art and Design's illustration program, Heather always thought her artwork was quirky and amusing, but the process of promoting herself as a freelancer was frustrating and discouraging. She has been surprised and heartened to know that her artwork in T-shirt form gets a positive reaction from people. "I don't think I really realized that I was capable of making humorous artwork until I started seeing people's reactions to my shirts," she says. "People will literally laugh out loud, sometimes very loudly, and it still amazes me. It's definitely rewarding when a customer or fan connects with the art and gets super excited—wanting to share the experience and making sure the friends they're with have noticed the particular shirt that has tickled their fancy. That's when it all seems worthwhile, and I feel like I'm having a positive effect on the lives of others."

"I do have a particular best-selling design that people seem to find hilarious and identify with my company. It's a simple drawing of an octopus who is frowning, accompanied by the text, 'I am sad because I only have seven arms.' People will literally laugh out loud upon seeing it and almost always make sure whoever they're with has also noticed it. It's the oldest design that I continue to reprint, but people still love it and continue to buy it!"

The graphics for a T-shirt begin as a doodle in her sketchbook. Heather lets her mind and hand wander on the paper: "When I draw, I don't usually have anything particular in mind, but prefer to put down a few random lines or shapes and then to just let my imagination take over from there." When a drawing tickles her fancy, she scans it, tests out various colour combinations and then prints it out at actual size. At this point, most silkscreen printers would use a light-sensitive photo emulsion to get the image on the screen, but Heather

instead traces the image onto a clear plastic sheet, cuts out the image with an X-Acto knife and then tapes the resulting stencil to the back of the screen.

"I started very low tech when I first learned, using three screens I made myself, and just placing the screens on the T-shirts by hand on a large board I wrapped with carpet underlay and an old bed sheet," Heather explains. "Over the past five years, I've been slowly adding equipment to make things more efficient and to increase my capabilities as a screen printer. I now have a four-colour printing press, a flash dryer and a lovely new conveyor dryer—one of my best purchases yet!—but I still silkscreen each shirt myself, by hand. The use of stencils gives my shirts a unique aesthetic and the water-based inks a more textured, vintage-like feel."

Adding to the unique quality of her products, she also pulls from a collection of vintage fabrics to add appliqué and other sewn touches to shirts and sweaters.

Her work is most definitely—and proudly—homemade. "My parents have graciously allowed me to set up in the greater part of their basement. It's where I have all of my screen-printing equipment and supplies, and where all the printing magic happens!" she says.

Once inventory is stocked up, Heather does not stay put for long. In a beloved 1971 VW camper van she's named Berthold (Bert for short), Heather takes her silkscreened magic on the road to handmade markets and festivals across Canada: "It's a highlight of the year because I get to spend a good part of the

summer outside, travelling around, listening to awesome music and meeting great people. It seems to be a really good fit for my shirts, too, as I've found that the kind of person attending a folk music festival has an appreciation for the arts and often a quirky sense of humour and an outlook on life that mirrors my own. I've found that my shirts definitely speak to a certain kind of person, having more to do with their sense of humour than with their age or gender."

- • WEBSITE *mumbletease.com*
- • SHOP *etsy.com/shop/mumbletease*
- • TWITTER *@mumbletease*
- • INSTAGRAM *@mumbletease*

*"I believe that as long as you continue learning in life, whether it be through reading, study, nature, taking workshops or good conversation, that the inspiration will find you."*

EVA SCHROEDER

# EVA SCHROEDER

CANBERRA, AUSTRALIA

Born to German parents who individually emigrated to Australia in the 1950s, met in Canberra and married there, Eva Schroeder says her childhood and teenage years were filled with hard work, creativity, music and imagination. "However, as is often the case with immigrants," she explains, "a great emphasis was placed on higher education leading to a good career. Creativity, at the time, was not seen as a possible way to achieve a secure financial future." Eva became a primary school teacher, but after nearly a decade teaching, she realized it was not where she was meant to be. And so she began her search.

"Over the past 20 years or so I have been searching for my space in the world and my journey has been varied," she says. "I have played the viola in two orchestras, one in Canberra and another in Japan. I have studied graphic design and worked in a Japanese design company—falling in love with handmade paper and gorgeous packaging on the way—lived through the great Kobe earthquake, worked on Japanese radio as an Australian announcer, and then on my return to Australia had to decide whether to work as a designer or on radio." She ended up at a sports and racing radio station where she worked a few years in marketing, looking after sales staff and creating ads. Eventually, she was offered a half-hour time slot in which her mission was to introduce the arts to sports and racing enthusiasts.

Her daughter was born, and during her maternity leave, Eva decided to follow her passion for paper: "I took up studying bookbinding as a hobby, which eventually led to experimenting with the sculptural capability of paper, an exhibition, and finding 'my thing.'" Ever curious, Eva is currently studying photography, particularly the beauty of black-and-white film photography and the process of developing images. "Eventually I would like to combine everything that I have learned within the creative sphere and bring it all together," she says.

"The satisfaction I gain from creating a physical object out of a concept or image in my head surpasses all other feelings. I find the whimsical world of paper art deeply satisfying—not at all useful, but imaginative and thought provoking. And as an added bonus, it invites others to share in my quaint world and understand a little of how I think."

Her work is often created for specific exhibitions, with specific themes. This helps focus and set parameters to the work. "It automatically sets a train of thought in motion," Eva says. "Often, I will do some domestic ironing with pen and paper close at hand, and the meditative back-and-forth motion seems to create a huge flow of ideas. If I am not interrupted, I can often gain the complete visualization of a piece. I then quickly write or a draw a description or sketch so that it is not forgotten. I often get many ideas at the same time and allow them to sift for a while. One firm idea

generally rises to the top and then the work begins—researching, collecting materials, experimenting and then finally creating. Sometimes it can take up to three months to make one piece."

The length of time required to create something is in part due to her divided attention and multiple responsibilities: "I have always felt envious of those artists/makers who could, in the midst of domestic chaos, hide away in their bedrooms and produce something beautiful in five minutes. I have visual diaries filled to the brim with ideas, quick thoughts and sketches, but need my husband at work, my daughter at school, the beds made, the domestic chores completed and silence for my best work to be produced."

Art making can be messy business, and Eva has an honest perspective on the fallacy of pristine-looking studios. "Whenever I see the beautifully organized workspaces of other creatives I sigh and then make a resolution to clean up!" she says. "My workspace, when I can actually get in there, is the three-by-

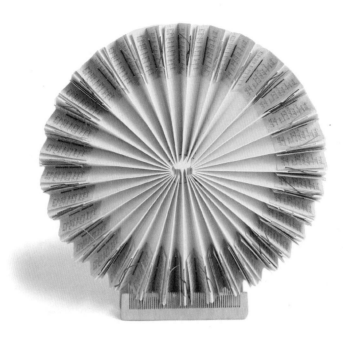

three metre third bedroom in our small house, and acts as my studio/office/creative space/ dumping ground." Underneath it all, she did create a custom environment: "I wanted it to be slightly mysterious and to look a little like a clearing in a forest. I painted the walls and ceilings green, had blinds and curtains made using textiles that contained leaves, and had a carpenter, using a variety of timbers, create trees and shelving to my design. I also wanted the feeling of a forest canopy, so I strung many whimsical items across the room." That was a number of years ago now, and Eva jokes, "Currently I can't see the trees for the paper. I am surrounded by books, inspirational magazines, images, cute creatures and piles of bits and pieces." Sometimes she works on the kitchen table when she needs a bit more elbow room.

Eva is currently working on her first solo exhibition, an effort that will combine paper art with black-and-white photography. It will be an installation that creates a dimensional experience for the viewer: "My work often contains layered meanings. It gives me the greatest pleasure to see the public view my pieces, and then hear them laugh with wry amusement as they understand my word play and the hidden messages."

Eva confesses that she is still not quite satisfied. "I have *so many* aspirations, am already middle-aged and know that I have fewer years ahead than behind. Sometimes I feel incredibly frustrated that I wasted so many years searching and that it took me so long to focus, and I envy those who specialize in their area of craft and become well known in their field of expertise. However, on the other hand, I have come to the realization that I need, and have, a wide variety of interests and will just have to continue searching for ways to combine them all."

133

# FIONA CHANDLER

FRESHWATER, NEW SOUTH
WALES, AUSTRALIA

"It was almost a midlife crisis but instead of a red sports car it was cadmium red ink and tubes of watercolour," says Fiona Chandler from her home in Freshwater, Australia. Some 20 years ago, Fiona completed a visual arts degree but veered away from drawing and painting to become a designer. "I sold out," she says, tongue in cheek. "I became a designer with some fabulous jobs with creative people."

As business expanded, she found her work less and less creative. On advice from her husband—"live a creative life, the rest will follow"—Fiona gave herself a year to explore other options. "I read and rang people. Artists who had done what I was hoping to do. People were so generous with their time and information. I wanted to be a part of this group of creatives," she says of her quest for creative fulfillment.

"Teaching was a great start with immediate feedback from students."

"I do think people are turning to what makes them happy—making a decision to step back from former careers or jobs and exploring their passions." She made the switch in 2012 and has discovered that success follows passion. "I paint because I can't *not*," she says. "After years as a designer the need to create without a brief was overwhelming—to channel the joy and release I feel when painting. My paintings are full of detail. I want the viewer to step closer to the artworks and discover something new each time."

Energized by the natural world around her, she creates joyful florals with splashes of watercolour: "People often ask about the colour and movement in my works. Leaves, sticks, flowers, bugs and bloom feature prominently. The happiness created when surrounded by nature, its many forms and colours, I try to capture that on paper." Fiona collects objects from nature on her walk to the studio at Warringah Creative Space, where she is an artist in residence: "Nature is the key for me. It might be a bloom, a seed pod or a fabulously shaped stick that begins my tangent."

The Warringah Creative Space is inspiring in itself. "Originally a disused Scouts hall, the building has been rebuilt using recycled materials, and houses four studios, a gallery and an edible garden. It is a creative hub for the northern beaches where I live," Fiona says. It is light and airy, with quiet mornings for con-

templative art making (the possums, she says, make a racket on the roof in the evenings). "The studio is a five minute bike ride through the park from home, so I often lay down a wash and leave it to dry in the early morning and pop back throughout the day. As an artists in residence, it is the first time I have had a studio just for painting. It is a treasure I am going to find very difficult to leave."

For Fiona, the most challenging thing about life as an artist is the financial side. Placing a value on one's art is difficult, as is opening yourself up to possible rejection. "I do sell my art," she says. "It has taken years, but now I do. I have been lucky to have a few people who ask to pop by and see what has been created. These sales keep me going. It's so very difficult to stand in front of something you have created knowing it is for sale. You feel truly bare. Once they leave there is much happy dancing and excitement. The energy to create is once again fuelled!"

- **WEBSITE** *fionakate.com.au*
- **INSTAGRAM** *@fionakatesimplegorgeous*

# FELICIA SEMPLE

MONTMORENCY, VICTORIA,
AUSTRALIA

"My process is a combination of necessity: a kid needs X, the materials—what do I have on hand?—and a form, either improvised or using someone's pattern," says Felicia Semple.

"Those three things wander around in my head until I can see what I need to make." Felicia doesn't sell her work, instead she makes functional objects and clothes for family and friends: "Part of the ongoing rituals of our daily life." Birthdays, Christmas, going back to school—these are all occasions for which to create.

In 2014, Felicia, her partner and their three small children flew from their home in Australia to the UK, and then over four months they travelled from Denmark down through Eastern Europe, ending in Greece. She purchased some yarn in Suffolk County, England, and with a "please, mama," one of her children coaxed her into creating a cardigan. "Because we were travelling with no access to books and little access to wifi, I had to improvise. I ripped it out many many times to get it right," she says.

"I knitted through Germany, Austria, old Yugoslavia and Albania. The steek was crocheted in Greece and the centre of the cardigan was finally cut open at a campsite in Umbria, Italy. I knitted the button bands in the UK before we flew home, and finally put buttons on upon our return home to Australia."

As the creator of The Craft Sessions, a creative space focused on bringing together people who craft for joy and on fostering a love of handmaking, Felicia is a strong advocate of crafting as a part of life. Her own work focuses on traditional, domestic handcrafts, which includes knitting, sewing, quilting and embroidering. "I believe you can make beautiful things with simple techniques and a pared-back style," she says. "I believe in simple."

She describes herself as coming from a long line of domestic crafters: "My mother was a sewing teacher and taught me to sew when I was tiny. She showed me how to take something I drew on paper and create a garment, helping make my dreams a reality. Her encouragement gave me confidence to believe I could make anything. I didn't touch craft during my 20s, but like many women before me, after having children I rediscovered my passion for making. I made for the joy of creating something tangible in the midst of the mainly invisible work that is daily mothering." The Craft Sessions began as a blog, as a way to encourage others in their making, spreading the positive, common-sense messages about the joyful side of making: that mistakes are how you learn that practice is how you get better, and that we all have the capacity to create.

"I write about the head stuff that we all go through when we are making," Felicia says, "about getting stuck, about the trap of perfectionism, that there is a difference between creativity and talent, and that you don't need to be talented to make out of pure enjoyment—and

about confidence and inspiration and being intentional in our making."

The comments she receives are a major highlight of the blog. "Really smart, thoughtful people seem to read what I write, and through their comments I get to learn more about whatever I have written," she says. "I love the creative feedback loop the blog has created. As a non-writer, the feedback to the blog has been a pretty big thrill. The response I had to a post I wrote about crafting through grief called 'Craft as a manifestation of love and loss' was particularly satisfying. I'm so glad I put it out there (after a long time of thinking I should) and I'm so glad people connected with it. It really does feel like community."

That sense of community spawned a retreat as well (also called The Craft Sessions), which provides not only new skills to both beginners and old-school crafters, but also an opportunity to connect with others over crafting. This retreat is now in its third year (as of September 2015) and offers workshops in quilting, knitting, lace, dyeing, sewing, weaving, embroidery and more.

"Through the blog, and social media like Instagram, it has become a community of online makers who share a love of handmaking," says Felicia. "So many good things have come out of this! It's all about the joy!"

- **WEBSITE/BLOG** *thecraftsessions.com*
- **TWITTER** *@thecraftsession*
- **INSTAGRAM** *@thecraftsessions*

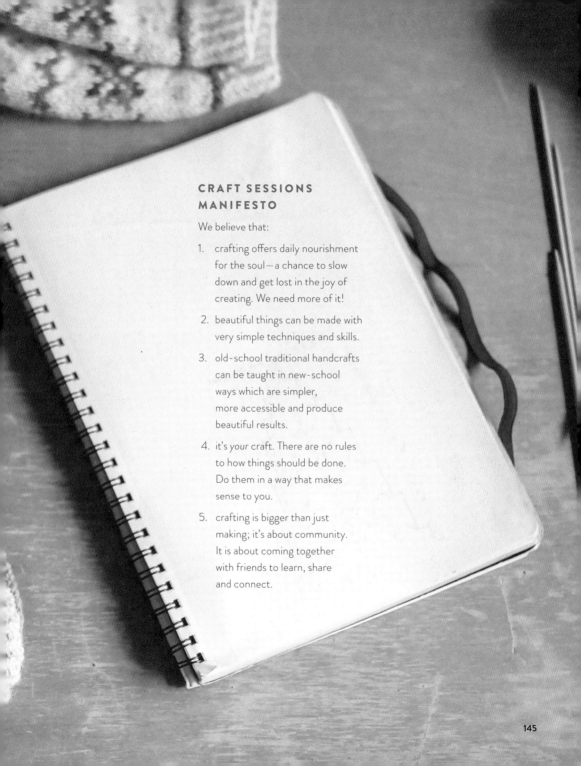

## CRAFT SESSIONS MANIFESTO

We believe that:

1.  crafting offers daily nourishment for the soul—a chance to slow down and get lost in the joy of creating. We need more of it!

2.  beautiful things can be made with very simple techniques and skills.

3.  old-school traditional handcrafts can be taught in new-school ways which are simpler, more accessible and produce beautiful results.

4.  it's *your* craft. There are no rules to how things should be done. Do them in a way that makes sense to you.

5.  crafting is bigger than just making; it's about community. It is about coming together with friends to learn, share and connect.

# KIM EICHLER-MESSMER

KANSAS CITY, KANSAS, USA

Raised in Iowa by parents who valued hard work, honesty, creativity and resourcefulness, Kim Eichler-Messmer had an early, first-hand education in craft entrepreneurship.

"My father was a carpenter when I was small and later changed careers to help my mother manage the small local newspaper she started and ran for many years. Due to a lot of hard work and some good timing, both of my parents were able to retire when I was in grade school and they both took up hobbies: my father created hand-painted and pieced wooden quilt wall hangings and my mother learned and mastered stained glass." With these new-found second careers, they set up studios in their home and sold work in regional shops and on the craft show circuit, and also sold stained glass supplies. "My parents trusted my (young, developing) taste enough to let me help choose colours and designs for their projects, and they also let me help track sales and inventory, and set up and tear down at craft shows."

In her post-secondary odyssey, Kim started in engineering before leaving for Spain to study abroad for one summer. She then changed

her major to Spanish with a minor in Portuguese. "After about a year as a Spanish major, I realized what I really loved about being in Spain wasn't the Spanish—it was the art. So I changed majors again to focus on drawing and printmaking," says Kim. "I was still rather confused about what I was good at and what I enjoyed doing, so I took classes in every medium offered at Iowa State, including ceramics, jewellery, furniture and textiles. The textiles classes combined everything I loved—the ability to draw and print on fabric with dye, and the tactility and problem solving of creating something by hand. Even though it took me a while to figure out my path, all of the confused steps along the way have influenced what I do and how I approach my work."

Looking back, Kim can see that growing up with parents who were makers paved the foundation for her own creative career. "I'm a maker first because it's in my blood," she says. "If my hands aren't busy doing something, I go a little crazy. I'm also a maker because it satisfies so many different needs in my life. I need to be productive, I need to be surrounded by beautiful, functional things, and I need to figure things out. Quilting offers up plenty of opportunities for problem solving. It's challenging and continuously tests my skills. It is also the best way I have found to express my ideas visually. I have tried nearly every art form and nothing else felt as natural to me as quilting."

"I dye fabric and make quilts that are inspired by colour theory, geometry and landscape. My landscape quilts are all one of a kind and attempt to capture the quality of light and sense

of place particular to the American Midwest. I also love to create custom landscape quilts for people inspired by places they love. I also love to dye fabric and come up with my own custom dye recipes. Many of my quilts explore the wide range of colour possibilities from dyeing gradations of colour."

When creating her landscape quilts, Kim starts with a time and a place. She studies the nuances of the light, the geometry of the land and the gradations of the sky. When she is out in the countryside, she documents the environment quite simply by using her camera phone. "I try to match up the feeling I get from a place with a visual photographic reference to use as a starting point," she explains. "From that initial feeling and photo I begin to dye fabrics that capture the quality of light and mood of the

place. Then I start sketching with fabric. I use a lot of improvisational piecing to create different aspects of landscapes. Because I am from the Midwest and currently live there, farms and fields are huge influences in my work. I create quilts almost like a collage—constantly putting fabrics together, stepping back to see how they work and reworking things until the quilt feels right."

Her quilts are works of art, and though she does sell her work, that is not her focus in their creation. "I learned that making work for the purpose of selling does not work for me," she says. "It stunted my creativity. So now I just make what I need to make and if it happens to sell I am happy."

Kim teaches workshops on fabric dyeing and quilting techniques, and also authored a book,

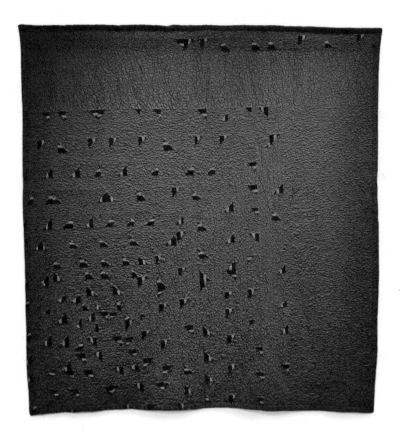

*Modern Colour: An Illustrated Guide to Dyeing Fabric for Modern Quilters.* "Writing the book was one of the hardest things I've ever done, but it was also one of the most rewarding," she says. "I'm currently working on writing quilt patterns and brainstorming ideas for another book. The quilts I created for my book and the patterns I'm working on now are very different from usual studio practice. They are much more rooted in traditional quilting and use commercial fabrics. It is a brand new challenge for me to come up with patterns that feel fresh and exciting, and to work within the constraints of commercial fabrics, but I'm really excited about the possibilities and the things I'm creating. I am starting to see how this change in thinking and working will feed back into my studio work and influence my landscape quilts."

In reflecting on her craft, Kim feels satisfaction in creating something special: "A lot of my quilts are a big struggle to get through. I'm not following patterns or prescribed rules; I'm trying to create an object that makes somebody feel something. So when I finish a quilt, hang it on the wall and I can feel that place, or someone else connects with it on a personal level—that is the best feeling."

- · WEBSITE *kimemquilts.com*
- · BLOG *kimemquilts.com/blog*
- · SHOP *kimemquilts.com/quilts-1*
- · INSTAGRAM *@kimemquilts*

*"I always have questions that need answering. Making a new quilt can bring up a whole series of questions that need to be answered by making other quilts. If I ever feel stuck or lacking in creativity I allow myself to just play with piecing and create for the sake of creating. Play and experimentation are incredibly important to me because they keep me excited and keep my skills sharp."*

KIM EICHLER-MESSMER

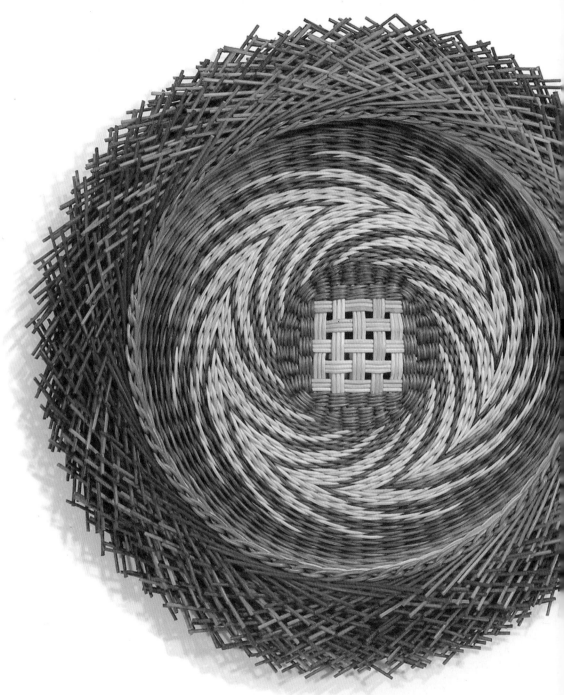

# KARI LONNING

RIDGEFIELD, CONNECTICUT, USA

Kari Lonning admits that she did not come to basketry out of an interest in basket making itself, but rather from her history in working with textiles and ceramics. "Weaving with rattan provides the best attributes of both: form in ceramics as well as structural techniques and patterning in textiles," she explains. "Colour, form and patterning are more important to me than traditional or functional baskets, or collecting my own materials. I've chosen rattan for its boring uniformity and its wonderful ability to take in dyes."

Kari grew up with parents who both held science degrees but nonetheless supported her artistic endeavours. She received a BFA in ceramics and textiles with a minor in metals, and soon after did her first craft fair: "In the early 1970s, I was part of a group doing craft fairs. We were hippy artists who liked making things with our hands as a way to express ourselves. These days, those of us who have been able to continue working in our respective media and have resisted the security of a 9-to-5 job are a sort of family. We get together a few times a year at fairs and recognize our shared histories. We may not be close friends, but as a family, we share a common bond."

Kari now lives in a Victorian house with an Old English Sheepdog named Emma and a stray cat named Kitt, who Kari says adopted them all three years ago. She finds inspiration in her garden and in the woods, where she loves to experiment with photography: "The light is different, the colours have changed, flowers have come into bloom or there's fresh snow on the ground. There is always something new to look at. All the visual information gets stored away in my brain to be drawn upon later."

She weaves in her kitchen, surrounded by plants, windows and neutral colours. "I work with very little clutter around me because I need room for all the new ideas as they emerge from of my head," she says. As she starts working with various shades of dyed reed, the room fills with experimental colour combinations.

"I like working with my hands, designing and

problem solving while creating something that didn't exist before I brought it to life," Kari explains. "I enjoy the process of weaving and the rhythm, the sense of discovery as the basket grows, the excitement and pride when it turns out just right. I love the infinite possibilities of being able to design and build objects and the freedom to make up an answer when I'm looking for a new solution. Experience has taught me the weaving techniques, so my hands are free to enjoy the repetitive process while my imagination is free to imagine future projects."

"I'm best known for my double-walled constructions and textural, 'hairy' baskets. I weave the double-walled pieces as two separate baskets, and add the glass marbles just before the baskets are woven together. I add the marbles for fun, but they add unexpected weight and sound when the pieces are handled. The hairy baskets came about because I wanted to make a better bird's nest. As I wove, I added dozens of short, multicoloured pieces into the weaving, so the nest would stay lodged in the branches, and be camouflaged. After experimenting with a number of little, hairy baskets, I began to play with more colour and went on to design baskets where the short pieces of reed created interesting, overlapping colour effects."

"Because so many people have preconceived ideas about baskets and basketry, they rarely pause to think about how different contemporary basketry and mass-produced, inexpensive, imported baskets are," says Kari. She started making her hairy baskets as a less-expensive basket with which to introduce possible future collectors to her work, but she also finds a creative advantage in them: "They gave me a way to experiment with riskier colour combinations without the time investment of larger pieces."

In 2000, she wrote *The Art of Basketry*, a book that not only shares her techniques, but also showcases the works of other basket weavers.

A couple years ago she started using encaustic, which added strength and rigidity to the bases of her baskets and allowed her to weave larger vessel forms and push the reed's structural constraints. In the future she contemplates an even more ambitious scale: "I would like to create large, outdoor installations and maybe collaborate with artists in other mediums, to work on projects that would exceed the physical constraints of working alone."

- **WEBSITE** *karilonning.com*
- **BLOG** *karilonning.blogspot.com*
- **TWITTER** *@karibaskets*
- **INSTAGRAM** *@karibaskets*

SKY COLE

"Sometimes an idea is so strong that I forget to eat, or turn on the lights. Then I have to stop because I've worn out my hands. The down side of this freedom is that I can never get completely away from what I do. I'm always pushing myself, thinking about possibilities."

KARI LONNING

158

# JOANNE YOUNG

KITCHENER, ONTARIO, CANADA

For most of her life, Joanne Young has lived in Kitchener-Waterloo, Ontario. In December 1999, she retired after 32 years of teaching high school mathematics. But retirement was just the beginning: "I was only 55, young enough to train for a new career. I was determined to reinvent myself as a textile artist."

The following October, Joanne enrolled in a distance learning City and Guilds Patchwork and Quilting class offered by Opus School of Textile Arts in London, England. "This school was headed by Julia and Alex Caprara, but is now unfortunately defunct. After eight years of intensive training I completed both a certificate and a diploma in patchwork and quilting. The highlight of these studies surely was an assessment exhibition held at the Museum of London in 2004. I completed my studies in 2008 and since then I have been a practicing studio artist."

For the past 30 years, Joanne has lived in an old neighbourhood in a downtown section of Kitchener, close to a railway line and old factories. "When I had to do a major project for the diploma program, I started to investigate this neighbourhood with my camera," she says. "I was first attracted to rusting surfaces—rust on pipes, rust on trash cans, rust on cars. But I was really smitten when I came across a corner

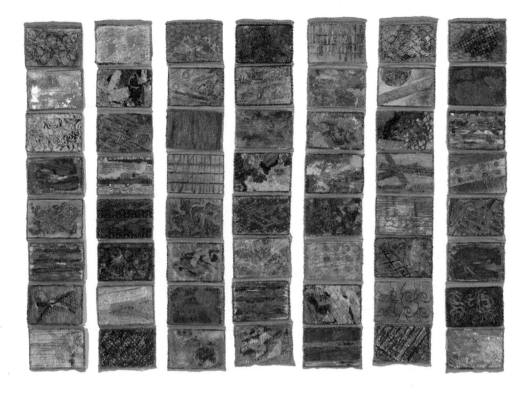

lot filled with bins piled high with metal scrap, part of a recycling yard."

Attracted to the colours, patterns and textures on the metal, her obsession with scrap resulted in a series of works: Scrapyard, Landfill, King of the Junkpile and Postcards from the Scrapyard. Raw edges, industrial-inspired colours and hand stitching make Joanne's textiles unique: "I make small to medium-sized wall hangings. They are made of various, usually natural fabrics, often hand dyed. For the past few years I have been dyeing fabric using tannin, from tea, and ferrous sulphate; this combination produces a grey that I find suitable for my theme of disintegration."

"The most fun was a piece called 'Scrapyard Couture by Bertold of Kitchener.' It consisted of two tiers: a large rusted spool that I had found in this recycling yard topped with a small roll of gutter wire. Sitting on the circumferences of these two levels was an assortment of handmade dolls. These dolls were about 12-inches high with heads sculpted out of paper pulp and bodies dressed by me out of bits and pieces of scrap. I had fun as this scrappy company of dolls grew on my worktable."

"Another section of the neighbourhood that intrigued me was the factory district. The old factories face the tracks; I could walk along the tracks and photograph the windows. Particularly those of the old Boehmer Box

Factory interested me; it has long ceased to make boxes and is now inhabited by artists and entrepreneurs who do not exactly decorate the windows but, let's say, make them graphic. So I left scrap behind for windows. I found that it is not easy to make windows and a wall interesting and spent almost a year making small pieces before I broke through with 'Colours of Abandonment,' which won an award."

As the city changes over time, Joanne adapts. Her neighbourhood is undergoing major changes, with many old houses being torn down: "I have moved on once more, this time to the theme of demolition. I am currently working on the third piece of a triptych titled, of course, 'Demolition.'" Ever attracted to surfaces

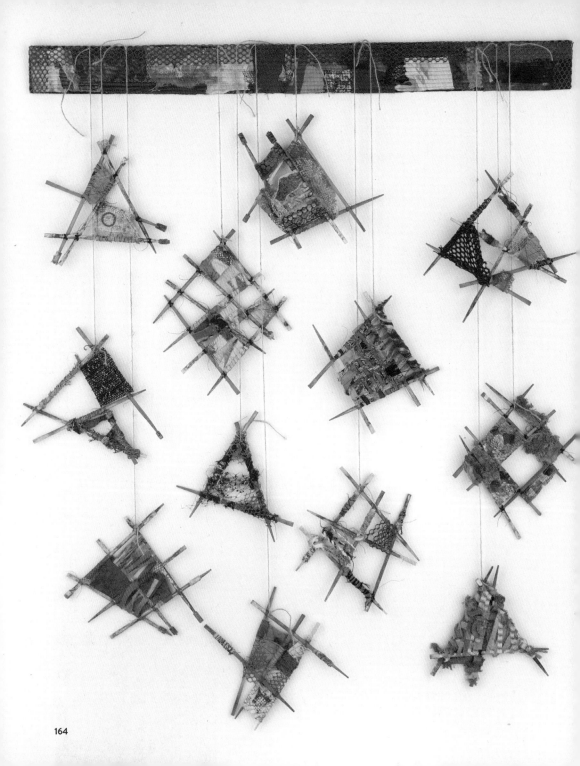

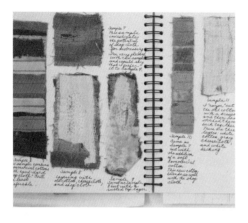

that show the wear and tear of life, Joanne's mission is to capture this beauty in her work.

Her process begins with photos taken around the neighbourhood, images that she studies for shape, colour and texture. "Next, I select a palette of colours from my stash to work with. Since I have been working with related themes for years, I have a large selection to choose from. Often to fill out my palette I will have to do some dyeing. Then I make samples—lots of samples. I learned this from my City and Guilds work and it is my most valued way to get into new work. As I make the samples, I absorb the subject matter, and then and only then do I start the work. The sample making takes a lot of time, but puts me in a dialogue with my materials so that I learn what they can and cannot do."

"I like the challenge of making," Joanne declares. "I like being surrounded by things I've made. I have read that you have to make for 10 years before you make things you like. Well, I've put in my apprenticeship and I do make things I like." She adds: "It's a bonus when you make things that others like as well."

# FLORA WAYCOTT

Flora Waycott can't recall a time when she was *not* making something with her hands: "It's something that has always lived inside of me that I couldn't ignore." When you are creative by nature, she says, the need to make is just part of who you are. "It is an extension of yourself and you can feel exposed and vulnerable sometimes because it is a little part of you that is in every piece that you make. When you are a maker, you are showing a very personal part of yourself to the world."

©flora waycott

"I like to do many different things: screen print, sew, paint, draw—and in each one of these I feel that my style comes through," says Flora. "I love nature, for example, and often in my work there will be leaves and flowers, and the occasional cat. It has become a bit of a running theme, but it really is very 'me' and shows what I love. I really do live up to my name!"

She was born in Southampton, England, to an English father and Japanese mother, and her family moved to Japan when she six years old so that she and her sister could experience their mother's culture: "Soon after we arrived, my parents bought me my first paint set and enrolled me in after-school art classes, where I would go once a week to draw, paint and make crafts with other children. I swapped stickers with my Japanese friends at school, collected pens and notebooks, and spent many hours

drawing in my sketchbook. The years we spent in Japan had a profound influence on me and played a huge role in shaping my creative path."

Flora's family eventually returned to the United Kingdom, where her English Granny, who was an embroiderer and smocker, influenced Flora's love of textiles in her teenage years. After graduating with a degree in textile design from Winchester School of Art, she worked as a designer in London making printed and embroidered textiles, then moved to New Zealand in 2008. Now she works as a freelance illustrator, represented by Lilla Rogers Studio. She also has a range of products that she hand makes, based on her illustrations.

"I make screen-printed tea towels, prints, giclée prints and cards from my illustrations," says Flora. "Illustrations can give you a feeling, a connection—it can awaken something inside of you or remind you of something special. I enjoy seeing if my illustrations will evoke these feelings in other people. I have all sorts of emotions when I am drawing, especially when I have created something I love and it is very personal to me. Your drawing of a cat will be different from mine because we interpret things in different ways. This really interests me."

Tea towels could be overlooked as domestic necessities, but in the right hands, a towel is a work of art: "I love tea towels and have always enjoyed collecting them and seeking out interesting designs. It felt natural to print my designs onto tea towels because of my passion for them. They are such a fantastic product—they serve a purpose and make an excellent gift—and can cheer up a kitchen and make you smile." As she screen prints the tea towels, Flora embeds a handmade, bespoke feeling into each one.

It is appropriate, then, that her tea towels are made in her home: "I work from home where I live with Nick and our cat, Shima. The spare room is my creative space, where I have my desk and computer, all of my books and my art materials. I have some inspiring pictures on the wall, tubs full of pens and other stationery and two bookshelves full of books and items I have collected from my travels. I often take my drawing into the living room, where light pours in from a large window and I can spread my work out on the big table as I look at the view of the sea."

For the messier work of printing, Flora heads to the garage: "It is a rental property so there are rules with what we could and couldn't do, but we have made the most of the space we have. We bought a small second-hand table for printing and covered it with thick canvas, with a few layers of a woollen blanket sandwiched between the canvas and the table to soften the surface for printing. Clamps are attached to the table to clamp smaller screens so they do not move, which I use when I print onto paper. There are shelves on the wall where I keep my pots of printing paste, inks, squeegees and other bits I need. I have about 10 custom-made screens that are stored in there and a washing

line that is strung across the length of the garage to dry the printed tea towels. We bought a second-hand bathtub from the recycle centre that I use to wash out my screens. The garage door is big and when opened fully allows good light to flood in."

Once the towels have dried on the line, they are heat pressed to set the ink. She takes care in packing them for her customers, using string and a little label for another personal touch. "Packaging may be my favourite part—folding the tea towels and stacking them up, ready for distribution, gives me such a satisfied feeling," Flora says. "I think that it is important to present your work well and pay attention to the little details—these are the things I notice when buying something handmade. I always try to give a little bit extra, like a well-placed label or an interesting sticker."

*"I love to support other creative people and enjoy doing creative swaps with friends and sharing their work with others. There is something about owning a product with a background story, which you know has had a lot of love put in it from start to finish. It feels so much more valuable to me."*

FLORA WAYCOTT

"I like to find beauty and inspiration in the little things, such as a small flower growing out of a crack in the wall or the contents of my kitchen cupboard. I live by the sea and I often go for short walks in my neighbourhood, looking for something to spark my imagination for my next project. As well as appreciating what is around me, I love to travel, and a trip away always brings fresh ideas and a full sketchbook." Flora returns to Japan once a year: "It is my other home, and I am never disappointed with the inspiration it offers. When I am away, I always discover fresh colour palettes and learn new directions to take my work in. When I return home, the small flower in the crack in the wall that I left behind is waiting for me and feels shiny and new again."

- WEBSITE *florawaycottdesign.com*
- BLOG *florawaycott.tumblr.com*
- SHOP *florawaycott.etsy.com*
- TWITTER *@florawaycott*
- INSTAGRAM *@florawaycott*

# KATHKATH STUDIO

English textile designer Kathy Schicker and Australian graphic designer Kathryn Pledger first met while pushing their respective prams in the south London district of Camberwell. Over talk of babies and motherhood, they discovered a shared passion in textiles. Together, they have formed KathKath Studio.

"We design surface patterns and produce high-end fashion accessories and products," they explain. "Our core product is a range of high-end silk scarves in the distinctive bright, bold and eye-catching studio style. The function of our scarves is to add that extra something to an outfit, and for the user to enjoy. Printed and hand finished in the UK, the scarves have the look and feel of classic hand-printed designs, with the luxury quality and feel of the best high-end scarf."

Trained in Jacquard weaving and with a specialization in innovative and light-reactive textiles for interiors, Kathy's work is driven by a fascination with light, new materials and the fusion of craft and new technology. Her work is research-led and is largely bespoke or collaborative. Kathy has an MA in Design for Textile Futures from Central Saint Martins and a BA in Visual Arts Textiles from Goldsmiths College.

Kathryn was born and raised in rural Australia, and her graphic design career has taken her across the world, recently focusing her love of colour and texture into producing surface pattern design. She has worked on many leading international household brands, designing identities, point of sale displays, exhibitions, print collateral and online resources. Her work is strongly influenced by her years of travelling and her love of hand-drawn elements, typography and photography. Kathryn has a BA (Honours) in Visual Communication from the University of South Australia.

"Our work is unique due to its bold colour and scale of graphics," the duo explain. "We sit in the

growing trend of high-end creative micro-businesses, who manufacture small collections and signature pieces for licence and for customers looking for an individual piece of artwork to wear. The digital manufacturing process, e-commerce and social media have opened this new market to us, and the landscape is changing and emerging all the time, so it is a very exciting moment to be part of this trend."

The pair works from Kathryn's home in South East London. "Our main office is the attic, our meeting room is the large kitchen table, and the workshop is in the shed on the side of the building," says Kathy. "We migrate and adapt! Neither of us are very neat, but once we've moved the toys out of the way, we function comfortably with our organized chaos." As

a team, they come up with themes of design briefs and then each work separately on the challenge. When they come together, they compare and discuss designs. "Then we collaborate on making the final design, often working on the same design together with different elements of each other's work."

"Inspiration for us is everywhere: fashion, art, graphics, nature, pattern, print, colour," they say. "London is an amazing city to live in, where inspiration can be found all around—from the street to world-renowned galleries. The hardest part is not being inspired, but deciding how to assimilate all that visual inspiration into collections! Working in a partnership helps to motivate us on a daily basis, as do our friends and family."

Selling online, at London fairs and in retail locations gets their products noticed, but the challenges in selling craft and creativity are numerous: "Finding the right locations to sell in the first instance is imperative. To make it work you have to have total confidence in your product so you can put yourself out there, which can be daunting but so important. Once you have new retailers it's a skill managing stock across several locations, and not getting lost in the crowd of all the other products. It's also a fine balance between being focused on your journey while remaining fresh and up to date. You have to constantly weigh your cash flow against being brave and taking risks."

"We have learned so much—making a product is just the start, you also need a strong narrative and professional images of your work for anything to sell. We have spent our first year selling a range of products in a range of locations, and that has informed us so much about what sells and why. We use that information to help us streamline and to make the difficult decisions about which designs and products to put into production, and which to leave behind."

- **WEBSITE** *kathkath.com*
- **BLOG** *kathkath.com/category/news*
- **SHOP** *kathkath.com/shop*
- **TWITTER** *@KathKathStudio*
- **INSTAGRAM** *@KathKathStudio*

# JOY LAFORME

PEARL RIVER, NEW YORK, USA

Joy Laforme has always been a creative person. "Any chance I had to work with my hands was a chance taken," she recalls of her childhood. "It was something I learned from my parents. I watched from a very young age as they repaired, designed, created and painted everything in our home. Like family, my creativity always grounded me."

In college, art was not a topic she thought of pursuing, but ultimately her creativity could not be suppressed: "I studied computer science, and even found a way to make that creative for myself as a web designer. My corporate experience after college was illuminating—I understood my strengths as an individual and in my ability to cultivate ideas on my own. I realized that I was meant to be an artist."

She began cultivating a portfolio of work by partnering with companies, clients and like-minded creatives. "When I eventually left

the corporate world to pursue a creative, entrepreneurial career to the fullest extent, my existence as an artist became crystal clear," she says. "I fell in love with textiles and illustration—and found that application of my work was the strongest and best work I had ever produced. The projects I have worked on have not always been glamorous, but they have all been fulfilling and notably instrumental to maintaining my career as an artist. I know that for me, this has only just begun."

As a textile artist and illustrator, she makes art that is applied to home decor, stationery and clothing. "I consider everything I create as an expression or emotional evocation of a season or memory—whether I am creating for a direct client, a textile studio who then sells my work to their clients, or a direct customer who purchases from my shop," says Joy.

Surface pattern design is a tricky business: trends come and go, and one must learn to adjust to the unpredictability of the market: "Patterns and colourful textiles have been popular in many cultures around the world for centuries, but trends can be daunting to grasp, as not everyone will love florals, geometrics,

conversational or minimalist prints constantly. Unpredictability can be frustrating—but it can also strengthen me as an artist, and more specifically as a business owner. The most rewarding thing is customers finding things I've designed and truly connecting with it. I am most rewarded and fulfilled when I have made my customers and clients happy."

"I recently spotted someone wearing a dress with a pattern I had designed through a textile studio a few years ago. In that moment, I knew that this person felt that the artwork on that dress was a creative expression of who she was. The design was something she had connected with, and was drawn to. I'm reminded of how good design will wrap itself around us like a dream or a memory. The image of something I have created to add brightness and joy to someone's life is the very reason I am passionate about what I do."

- **WEBSITE/SHOP** *joylaforme.com*
- **SHOP** *joylaforme.com*
- **TWITTER** *@joylaforme*
- **INSTAGRAM** *@joy_laforme*

*"The challenge of selling directly to a customer hinges on creating new and captivating pieces regularly while remaining true to oneself as an artist with a signature style. By nature it can be difficult to not compare your own level of success to someone else's— but understanding that what you do comes out of your own unique perspective is integral to staying grounded and creating original art."*

JOY LAFORME

# JACQUELINE CHAN

ORANGE, NEW SOUTH WALES, AUSTRALIA

"Although it might sound primitive to some people, I find the handmade process very rewarding and such a relief from all the mass-produced goods out there," says Jacqueline Chan from her home studio in Orange, a country town some 250 kilometres west of Sydney, Australia. "When I started my small business, I had minimal capital, so I started by making most of my products by hand and with whatever tools I had at home."

Under her brand Whimsy Milieu, Jacqueline makes a range of small items, from wooden rings, statement necklaces, block-printed pouches and cushion covers, to wallets and scarves: "All things that people can use or wear and feel happy about," she says. Her materials are wood, leather and natural textiles with which she makes quirky, colourful products. "They are really just for anyone who needs a dose of whimsy."

Jacqueline originally studied engineering in university, but it was her own search for creative whimsy that led to a switch: "A year into my first engineering job made me realize that I wanted to live a creative life and be happy. So I went back to university to obtain a degree in design, and subsequently started my small design studio, Whimsy Milieu."

All of her products are made in her second-bedroom studio in her home that she shares with her partner, a dog and a cat. "I design, draw, paint, sew, saw, cut, stitch, assemble and pack everything on my two trusty desks," she says. "I have two tall shelves filled with my books, inventory and supplies, and many boxes filled with more supplies and materials." Jacqueline loves to rearrange her studio furniture and wall of sketches and drafts. "It gets my creative juices flowing."

"My process often starts with an idea that just pops into my head or is sparked by something else that I saw. I then do some research and sketch many possibilities. More often than not, these lead to ideas that are different from my

*"The main challenge of selling craft and creativity is getting the customer to see and appreciate the value behind our goods. Consumers are so used to mass-produced products that are relatively cheaper, and oftentimes do not see or understand the time and labour we put into every single product."*

JACQUELINE CHAN

initial idea. At some point, I force myself to whittle down the possibilities and keep one or a few that I like and seem feasible. I then start to make prototypes or samples, and test drive them (sometimes I get impatient and cannot wait to get them into my online shop!). After a couple of rounds of refining the product, I then decide that it is ready to meet the world. I make a small batch, photograph them, and list them in my Etsy shop and promote them on social media."

She stays inspired by surrounding herself with books and magazines that she loves: "I also spend too much time ogling on Pinterest and design blogs. The fact that I can work from home—or anywhere if I have my tools with me—and be my own boss motivates me every single day. I wake up, enthusiastic about the day's work, and go to bed thinking about the many things that I can do to better my business."

- WEBSITE/BLOG *whimsymilieu.com*
- SHOP *etsy.com/shop/whimsymilieu*
- TWITTER *@whimsymilieu*
- INSTAGRAM *@whimsymilieu*

# JENNIFER ORKIN LEWIS

IRVINGTON, NEW YORK, USA

"I'm known for my daily sketchbook and the style I've developed while creating it," says Jennifer Orkin Lewis from her attic studio in an old village house north of New York City. "I paint a 30-minute painting a day and the looseness and intuitiveness of those paintings have become my signature. I love the feel of paint on the paintbrush laying down on paper."

Jennifer posts her daily sketchbook on Instagram to share with the creativity community. "My followers on Instagram and Facebook are so supportive and wonderful, I find that I'm inspired and motivated by everyone there," she says. "I've made friends through these communities whom I've met when I've visited new places. It's just wonderful how the world has opened up."

Having a daily creative routine with a sketchbook trains you to think creatively on demand—which for Jennifer is a very useful skill to have when it comes to her illustration commissions: "Many artists have been doing paintings a day; it keeps one's creativity in high gear. My sketchbook becomes a diary or journal of my life that I'm sharing with the world, and it opens up a meaningful dialogue with others. I see that kind of journaling, whether art or writing, as part of a larger trend. The

most challenging thing is coming up with new ideas every day, and it's also the most rewarding! Some days it feels almost impossible that I will create something new and interesting but somehow I just start and something emerges."

Jennifer's path to art and illustration was not quite a direct route. She originally studied textile design at the Rhode Island School of Design and was employed as a designer and stylist. "I saw lots of amazing art but was managing and curating rather than creating myself. I desperately needed to make my own work again and made a decision to become an illustrator," she says. "It was a slow road trying to find my style again. When I look back now I see what I did as a kid is closer to what I do now."

Jennifer reflects on her childhood, describing her household as "pretty loud and turbulent." Her mother was always exploring different creative paths and was a positive creative influence. Her father was a lawyer, but artistic as well: "I retreated to my room often and spent lots of time painting and drawing. I painted very intuitively on large paper with a lot of freedom. It was my happy place as a teenager."

Jennifer has a new happy place in her studio: "It has beautiful, rusty orange walls and a cute old rectangular window that looks over the trees. I have three desks: a stand-up one for painting, a sit down one also for painting and the other for my computer, printer and scanner. There is also an area with an easel for larger paintings. It's a very cozy, warm space. I spend most of my time up here and it's all my own."

She sells prints of her work on Etsy and recently signed on with artist agent Jennifer Nelson. "Now I have an agent to do my marketing to companies for licensing to manufacturers, and

getting me work for editorial and publishing houses. This takes a huge burden off of me because this is most definitely my weakest point," Jennifer says. "Having an agent opens so many doors for me. I feel like I'm just at the beginning of a whole new career. I want to do more editorial illustration as well as license my work for amazing products."

"My detour was long but it influenced me greatly—and it brought me full circle to the art I love making."

- **WEBSITE** *augustwren.com*
- **BLOG** *augustwren.blogspot.com*
- **SHOP** *augustwren.etsy.com*
- **TWITTER** *@augustwren*
- **INSTAGRAM** *@augustwren*

# JOSEPHINE KIMBERLING

RENTON, WASHINGTON, USA

Josephine Kimberling spent more than a decade working in creative corporate environments—fashion and greeting cards—but from there she has taken an interesting path in finding her own creative voice and niche.

"Five years ago I decided to stop climbing the corporate ladder, and instead construct my own," Josephine says. "I've been working for myself these past five years and absolutely love the leap I've taken into licensing my art. This avenue has allowed me to do what I love most—create art for a variety of products instead of a single focus. I enjoy working with companies to beautify their products, and you can currently find my art on stationery, handbags, fabrics, wall art, rubber stamps, gift products and even cake! The endless scope of product possibilities also keeps me constantly learning and growing, which is detrimental to creativity."

Last year, she started painting again, something she hadn't explored since college. With the encouragement of a friend, she landed a show at her local Anthropologie store. "Having just started painting, it was illuminating to have my work recognized by a company I admire," she says. Her weekends were filled

with painting as she built up enough work for the show.

Now these paintings have become part of her creative and professional life, as she balances her pattern design and licensing business with selling prints. "The most challenging thing is adding another hat to my already full plate, and deciding what to say no to in my life, so I can make what I love most the priority," Josephine says. "Selling directly to the public is a whole other business model, and with licensing as my main focus, it's challenging to juggle it all."

However, she has found opportunities for the two to work together—part of her style involves incorporating her pattern work into her paintings. "Everything I use in my paintings, I create myself," she exlains. "I don't use vintage or scrapbooking papers by other artists; I create my own. And I hand make my own stencils. My painting style creates a world that combines optimism and daydreams with echoes of realism."

"A trend that's been making it's way down the pike and is here now is for artists to get back to traditional media, get messy and share that with the world," Josephine says. "Art created with the artistic hand is vulnerable and real and captivates people in a unique way. Our world has been craving that type of spontaneous happiness, and now it's time for artists to shine. I've been feeling this pull for a while, and giving into it has caused me to be a part of this larger trend. I find it refreshing because it's allowing me to utilize all of the tools in my creative toolbox that I've learned and cultivated over the years, and create something new with them."

Josephine divides her workspace between these two sides of her business and creativity: "My workspace is in my home. I have two large tables in my workspace—one is for my computer and printers, where I do my design work and left-brained activities, and my second table is a standing-height desk that I can paint and draw on and where all of my creative tools surround me. The graphic designer part of me enjoys a clean and organized space to work in so my mind can be clear and able to focus on the task at hand, so I like to keep things as organized as possible. I have a bookcase that holds many books, and flat files that store my drawings and sketches, collage papers and such."

Selling her high-quality giclée prints on Etsy has allowed her to be directly in touch with her customers: "With licensing, most of my business is done behind the scenes, and I was crav-

ing the interaction and feedback that comes with dealing directly with a consumer. I knew I wanted to find a way to bridge the gap. The most rewarding part is making a sale and hearing that the customer loves it! Nothing better than knowing that something you made truly inspired happiness in someone else."

This is a stark contrast to Josephine's corporate background. "When working in the fashion industry, I would show my work to buyers and get feedback as to what sells and what doesn't based on numbers and data," she explains. "This did inform my creativity, and caused me to gear my work more towards the commercial side. Being on the other end of that, it's informative to learn and give your customers what they are asking for. To fill a need and hole in the market. However, once you get away from your core and who you are

and what caused them to love you in the first place, it's dangerous ground. As artists we need to find the balance of maintaining our integrity while allowing sales and feedback to inform and grow us. But we need to hold everything that comes at us against the light of who we are and decide its weight before taking action."

- **WEBSITE** *josephinekimberling.com*
- **SHOP** *etsy.com/shop/josephinekimberling*
- **TWITTER** *@PatternSavvy*
- **INSTAGRAM** *@josephinekimberling*

# JULIE GUYOT

TALLAHASSEE, FLORIDA, USA

"My grandparents lived about a mile from their closest neighbour and they got together to socialize over food and service. Weddings, funerals, quilting circles and farm work all involved cakes, pies, casseroles and a lot of hard work," recounts ceramicist Julie Guyot from her home in Tallahassee, Florida. "What started out of necessity has now turned into the DIY movement. It was not a lifestyle that you chose; it was a life that you lived."

Her grandmother grew up in the south and moved to Illinois to marry her grandfather. Two generations later, Julie grew up in Central Illinois, surrounded by corn and soybean fields. About 10 years ago, she moved from the Midwest to the South. "This change in culture has had a big impact on my work," she acknowledges. Her nostalgic, pretty cups, berry bowls and vases are as beautiful as they are useful. "I predominately make functional ceramic pieces. I focus on serving pieces and small, versatile gift items."

Adorned with vintage-inspired florals, patchwork-like decoration and elements of calligraphy, her work is a marriage of surface and shape. "Many people tell me that they've never seen pots like mine before," she says. "I used to be known for silk-screening onto my clay, but lately I've been putting my drawings onto my pieces in a process that requires three to five firings. Most ceramic work is only fired twice, but my technique takes a little more patience, time and labour to build the layering effect that I want to achieve."

Julie describes the process from start to finish: "It can take weeks to design a new piece, but once it's designed, I use either a tar paper template or a bisque mold to cut my shapes out of a slab of clay. I do not throw on a wheel; all of my work is hand built, mostly with slabs or coils. It is time consuming but I love building this way. I either decorate by painting on coloured slips and then painting the piece in a clear glaze or I dip the piece in a coloured glaze. The piece is fired twice and then my

"One of the most challenging aspects about a life in craft is figuring out how to make a living. The other difficulty is that your work is such a reflection of yourself that you are constantly thinking about how it can be better or designed differently or how your work can continue to make people happy. It's very personal."

JULIE GUYOT

drawings are painstakingly applied in the form of a laser decal that I print out. The piece is fired again and might get an additional decal that is custom made for me or a commercial decal that is readily available. Another firing is necessary to make all the imagery permanent."

The investment of time and patience into each piece speaks to her appreciation of heritage. Fortunately, she has a customer base willing to invest in the process. "My customers know that they are receiving an heirloom piece that can be passed down to their family," she says. "I think that getting back to a slower culture is a trend that many people are seeking out. People seem to appreciate the handmade object and the small craft business right now and there is less education that has to be done to find our audience."

Julie sells her work in different venues, depending on the type of work. Her sculptural work is shown and sold through galleries, typically as part of a curated or thematic exhibition. "I also have functional work in several galleries across the country. These are usually one-of-a-kind, higher-end pieces," she says. "I also have a line of work that I consider to be production work that is sold in shops." Balancing these three lines has been challenging: "I've recently been re-evaluating these venues to see how I can sell more work but still get my name out there and still make pieces that are exciting for me. Right now, I'm focused on building my business for the next few years. I feel like I'm shifting away from making every piece one of a kind and moving more toward production."

To a certain extent, selling her work affects what she makes: "When I decided that I wanted to focus on increasing my sales, I really had to take a look at expanding my audience and found myself asking what appeals to a larger audience. Even though I like work that is really colourful and that contains a lot of imagery, more neutral tones work better in most people's homes, and these objects are also more easily gifted."

This year, Julie began renting a studio space, her first in a decade and a half. It is one of 15 little cottages built in the 1920s that were formerly a motor inn at Lake Ella in Tallahassee in the 1970s. "It is 10 times the size of my previous home studio and is in an area where people can park and walk from shop to shop," she says. "I now have a retail area where I can sell my work. This new studio space has greatly increased my production and efficiency. It is amazing."

"The most rewarding thing about a life in craft is that I get to go to work every day and make things! I get to hear how a berry bowl that I made is making someone eat healthier. I get to create a mug that someone will use every day as they have their morning tea. I get invited into people's lives with the objects that I make. I feel a real connection with my community."

- **WEBSITE** *julieguyot.com*
- **INSTAGRAM** *@julieguyot*

## ON THE CRAFT OF SANDWICHES

Julie once had a job making sandwiches at a health food store. "One day I realized that I was taking a long time putting lots of love into my sandwiches and making the best-looking, well-packaged product. I knew it had been too long since I had made art. But my sandwiches looked good!"

"Craftsmanship manifests itself in many ways. The only thing I was ever really good at was creating. I discovered clay in college but stuck with it mostly because clay people are so giving and supportive. If I ever had to give up clay I would certainly find another medium to create with but I would really miss my people."

# JUNI TAN

MIAMI, FLORIDA, USA

Unlike many creatives, Juni Tan did not start drawing at a young age, and instead grew to appreciate the visual arts as a teenager: "Having no prior experience or training as a child, I considered myself a talentless admirer and contented myself with art history classes instead of picking up a pencil to try it for myself." By the time it came for her to apply to college, however, there was no doubt in her mind that she wanted to attend art school. "I sketched and practiced as much as I could to put together a portfolio for my college applications. Looking back, my portfolio was weak, but I am proud of how I overcame my self doubt to give it my best shot."

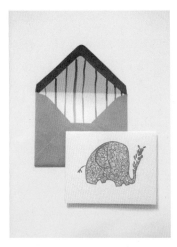

She moved from Singapore, where she had grown up, to New York to attend the Pratt Institute, immersing herself in formal art and design classes for the first time. "My printmaking classes were the most life-changing. I found them to be the perfect blend of fine art and design," she says. "Three months after beginning silkscreen classes, I started Hej Juni, my Etsy shop of silkscreen goods designed and made by me."

Juni is currently taking a break from college and has a day job in corporate marketing, so she dedicates evenings and weekends to her fledgling paper goods business. "My bedroom is transformed into a makeshift studio when I get home from my day job," she says. "Silkscreens, jars of ink and squeegees are brought out so I can roll up my sleeves and get to work. It's not exactly glamorous, and although a dedicated studio space would be ideal, I'm happy to do what I can at the moment to keep honing my craft."

Some might assume that keeping one's craft to the fringes of the day would be exhausting, but for Juni it is invigorating: "When I print, I go into my own little bubble where it's just me and my art. In the past few years, I've moved across continents a lot, started college, taken a break from college, started and left jobs, and even gotten engaged and married. Hej Juni is one of the few parts of my life that hasn't been tossed in the air and shaken up. There have been moments when other areas of life got too stressful, and I considered closing up shop to give myself some breathing room. But

I kept at it because I knew the opposite is true: designing and silkscreen printing doesn't add to my stress, it relieves it and keeps me sane."

Juni sees the current trend of craft revival from two perspectives. On one hand, the new appreciation given to analog pursuits was her introduction to printmaking: "I'm proud to stand amongst many silkscreen printers who are breathing new life into an age-old craft. Letterpress, silkscreen, block printing are just a few of the printmaking methods that are enjoying a revival and many new modern fans." Conversely, she views a trend toward highly curated art and craft lifestyles with some trepidation. "Lifestyle curation is ruling the world these days," Juni observes. "I see my work as an anti-heroine in that sense. With its loud colours, childlike details and little silkscreen imperfections, my work is miles away from fitting into perfectly styled moody and minimalist photoshoots. I find it sad that nowadays, it's considered fashionable to have a 'curated' life. People curate their clothes, their food, their furniture, everything. There's nothing wrong with having style and taste, but a lot of people seem to have forgotten how to relax and have fun. I strive not to take myself too seriously; it's important to be a little rough around the edges and have fun—I like to think that my work represents these values, and that they'll help bring much-needed smiles and childlike wonderment."

Her products are illustrated with kawaii animals like bunnies and little elephants. "I love adding little details like clothes, moustaches and hats to give them more character and personality," she says. Each card or gift wrap is screen printed by hand, and she paints each envelope liner for her greeting cards with watercolour, a time-consuming and laborious touch, but something that makes her proud.

With light-hearted messages and silly puns, it can be difficult for others to appreciate the hard work and effort that goes into her products: "My biggest challenge is getting skeptical loved ones to see that craft isn't just a silly hobby that's all play and no work. Some of them have difficulty seeing it as a viable career for me. Although this (thankfully) does not diminish the joy that I get from creating, it does get tough when you don't feel the full support of your nearest and dearest behind you." Despite this, Juni has persevered with what she loves. She resolved to remove the word "timid" from her vocabulary and has faced challenges head on, and is moving closer to her dream of working on Hej Juni full time.

"The most rewarding moments happen when I see even the most sullen of faces crack a smile at the silly puns on my greeting cards. It makes me want to pump my fist in the air and do a victory dance! My craft makes me incredibly happy, but even that can't compare to making others happy."

- WEBSITE *hejjuni.com*
- INSTAGRAM *@hejjuni*

### DIGITAL VERSUS
### THE HARD WAY

In selling handmade paper goods, Juni has a lot of competition. Not only are greeting cards and wrapping paper readily available, it is hard to compete with mass-produced or digitally printed stationery. "There are plenty of great stationery designers out there who choose to print their work digitally," says Juni. "Digitally printed cards and gift wrap have a much lower production price, and therefore a much lower sale price. It can be frustrating to lose customers for price reasons, but it's important to keep in mind that the hard work and love that goes into silkscreen printing can't be negated for the sake of a sale. I would be selling myself out and being unfair to other handmade stationers. On the flip side, I deeply enjoy meeting customers who appreciate my labour of love, and am also incredibly honoured when people choose my designs over cheaper alternatives." Juni holds onto a motto she learned while studying at Pratt: "Be true to your work and your work will be true to you."

*"When I print, I go into my own little bubble where it's just me and my art."*

JUNI TAN

*"The most rewarding moments happen when I see even the most sullen of faces crack a smile at the silly puns on my greeting cards. It makes me want to pump my fist in the air and do a victory dance! My craft makes me incredibly happy, but even that can't compare to making others happy."*

JUNI TAN

"I work on paper because I'm in love with its texture and surface."

MARY O'MALLEY

# MARY O'MALLEY

ROCHESTER, NEW HAMPSHIRE, USA

Mary O'Malley creates highly detailed ink drawings on paper, often with metallic inks on velvety black paper. This reversal, of putting lighter inks on a dark background, emphasizes the complex detail and ornate patterns in the drawing. "The labour-intensive nature of my work is important to me, as it serves as a type of meditation that I find necessary to my well-being," she says.

She is inspired by natural motifs such as florals, birds and insects, and describes the designs as "intricate tangles that resemble chandeliers or bouquets."

"I've lived in the Northeast United States my whole life, where the change of seasons is a big part the everyday. It's still exciting to me to witness the slow thaw from winter to spring, or to feel that first tinge of fall in the air. This fascination with nature and natural cycles serves as a starting point for my work, combined with my love of pattern, ornament and decoration. Flora and fauna, obsessive patterning and a Baroque sensibility come together to create a new world of hybrid chandeliers, curious bouquets, dense gardens and imagined landscapes that exist somewhere between the extravagant lushness of nature and the rigorous orderliness of lace patterns."

Her motivation is to go deeper than surface-level: "I am interested in a kind of beauty that is boldly decorative, unapologetically pretty and aggressively feminine."

She tries to stay away from trends, relying on her own instincts about the images that she produces. "That being said, I am extremely interested in all aspects of visual culture, whether it be art and design, fashion, film or craft. I'm always scouring the Internet, magazines and sites like Pinterest for visual stimulation, so I'm sure some trends do seep into my work and subconsciously become an authentic part of my visual language," she admits. "I think my work fits into a recent resurgence of drawing

and the handmade art object, as people crave a respite from the slickness of our digital world, and turn towards something more human and imperfect."

She works at home, where it is cozy and comfortable. "I like to think of it as my laboratory, with all my tools and books and inspiring objects around me while I work," she says. "I sit at a large table with everything I need at arm's length. My studio is also somewhat of a library, with my collection of art books and reference material nearby, and of course a comfy chair for reading. I also keep my collection of natural found objects—bones, feathers, shells, stones, etc.—in my studio, and display it on a rotating basis (it's too large to display all at once!). These objects are deeply connected to my work and serve as inspiration for many of my pieces."

She sells high-quality inkjet prints of her work on Etsy and sells originals and photo-lithographic prints via a Big Cartel shop: "These two venues have opened up my work to new audiences, and has allowed me total control of how my work is presented. I like how these online shops can empower someone who is perhaps new to buying art or does not have access to a gallery. I also sell work through more traditional means, such as galleries and art consultants."

"Making reproduction prints of my work has led me to think about other applications of my work, such as pattern and surface design," says Mary, who hopes to develop some repeat

patterns for wallpaper and fabric. "I'm also working on ways of incorporating three-dimensional elements into my work, such as embroidery and beading."

Mary knows the trials of balancing making art with other obligations: "The most challenging part of being any maker or creative person is trying to balance making your work with the rest of your life, whether that is family, other work or both. The long solitary hours and focused concentration necessary to make my work competes with my need to earn an income and nurture relationships with loved ones and friends. It's a daily challenge to strike the right balance."

"The most rewarding part is watching this visual world that I've created transform and grow over the years. When what I've made touches another person and brings them joy or meaning, or challenges them in some way, I know I've done my job."

- **WEBSITE** *maryomalleyart.com*
- **BLOG** *maryomalleyart.com/blog*
- **SHOP** *maryomalleyart.etsy.com*
- **TWITTER** *@maryomalleyart*
- **INSTAGRAM** *@maryomalleyart*

## ART AS EXERCISE

"Art making is a discipline; it's very similar to exercise: if you don't use it, you lose it," says Mary. "Good work usually comes out of your previous work—making begets making. I love the famous Chuck Close quote: 'Inspiration is for amateurs; the rest of us just show up and get to work.' Inspiration is not something you can wait around for, you have to find it, and if you can't find it you have to invent it. Sometimes you have to make yourself work when you really just want to take a nap or read a book. That piece that you make that feels like it just dropped out of the sky and made itself was actually the result of all your hard work, frustration, mistakes and failed attempts—so you have to just keep plugging along!"

# KIM
# ANDERSSON

KENSINGTON, CALIFORNIA, USA

With her joyful and fun fabric designs, surface pattern designer Kim Andersson is part of the resurgence of modern aesthetics bringing new energy to the quilting community.

Her debut fabric collection was launched in early 2015 through Windham Fabrics. With this collection, entitled Tidal Lace, Kim realized a dream that all surface designers have. "I must say, it feels so amazing to finally see and hold this collection. There have been a few (good) teary moments here," she says from her studio in San Francisco.

"I have a lifelong connection to sewing and textiles. My mother and grandparents really inspired me to start crafting, and by them taking the time to share their craft experience my interest was born." Six years ago, Kim and her family moved from Sydney, Australia, to San Francisco. "I was in awe of all the fabulous fabric and pattern books available here," she recalls. "Blessed with a new baby that slept (my first didn't), I bought a sewing machine and started to sew again. It was through wonderful quilting fabrics (Amy Butler, Denyse Schmidt, Anna Maria Horner) that my passion for fabric and textile design was reignited!"

This return to fabric came after schooling in visual communications and a career designing for the screen (TV and the Internet) in Australia. She was dissatisfied with the virtual and intangible: "I wanted to see my designs on something that I could hold and feel." Searching for the answer, she heard about the California School of Professional Fabric Design. "I knew that my sewing and quilting experience would help me to design a well-balanced fabric collection, so after some time at the fabric design school, I started I Adore Pattern and went for it!" A good friend and mentor, Carol Van Zandt, offered early support and advice as Kim developed her first collections and took them to Quilt Market, the quilt industry trade show.

"My fabric collections are sold in local retail and online fabric stores worldwide," Kim says. "I don't sell the quilts I make directly, but I've designed and made projects as part of the marketing push for my fabric collection. Prior to the launch of a collection, sample products are sewn to show off the possibilities of the new line. Part of the process of releasing the collection was working with Windham to produce the look book for the collection. I really enjoyed the process of planning the shoot and styling the shots; it was as if all my design experience was coming together into one package. I also had the support of an amazing friend, Danielle Collins, who took the photographs for me. We learned a lot through this process and were able to pull from both of our creative experiences. I've also been amazed at what people created with Tidal Lace for the look book. When I asked people to make a project for it I had no stipulations other than when I would need to photograph it, and they totally bowled me over with their creativity. Having the fabric out there feels like a collaboration with creative types that I have never met, so I'm really excited to see where people take Tidal Lace in their own projects."

Whether designing fabric or designing a quilt, Kim starts at the same place. "I begin with an inspiration point and then play around with technique and layout. I love the initial research part where I look through many images to find my jumping off point—it might be from a fashion shoot in a magazine, a photo from a family holiday or a squiggle I drew on a Post-it. Sometimes I get an idea and have to jot something down straight away before I forget it, sometimes it's a longer and evolving process. Once I hit on an idea that feels right I continue to iterate on it. I love that feeling of flow when everything connects and just works. Not that everything works, of course—there are starts that don't seem to lead anywhere. Still, I keep these starts because they may spark something else, or maybe it just isn't the right time for them. That quilt block may just be waiting for me to have a bit more experience before I can tackle it, or maybe I need to ask a friend about it to get that creative spark happening again."

Tidal Lace is an illustration of Kim's memories of exploring the beach with her grandparents. "I really enjoy designing fabric patterns with a story behind them," she says. "Sharing memories and experiences from my life makes them come alive." The wonderful part of creating fabric is that once it is in the hands of a new crafter, it becomes the first step in this person's creative journey. "Once someone has my fabric in their hands it's up to them what they want to create with it. I hope that my work has inspired them to make something wonderful. I love this connection and can't wait to see what people make with my fabric!"

What is her advice for someone starting out in fabric design? "Research and study what is out

225

*"Every time I turn on my sewing machine I'm excited to learn something new."*

KIM ANDERSSON

there—how are your designs unique? Look at fabric design through history, it's good to have an understanding of all the different pattern styles. If you can get a mentor, it's good to be able to throw ideas around with someone with design experience in the field that you want to get into. If you want to work with a fabric manufacturer, talk to other designers that work with them so that you have some understanding of how they work."

- **WEBSITE** *iadorepattern.com*
- **BLOG** *iadorepattern.com/blog*
- **TWITTER** *@iadorepattern*
- **INSTAGRAM** *@iadorepattern*

# MARIE-MICHELLE MELOTTE

CALGARY, ALBERTA, CANADA

Marie-Michelle Melotte was born and raised in Calgary, Canada, to parents who emigrated from their native island of Mauritius.

"I don't often talk about my father, maybe because he's such a quiet, gentle and constant presence in my life," reflects Marie-Michelle. "My father is a skilled craftsman who works with metal primarily and sometimes with wood. He is a perfectionist and can make just about anything by himself and with his own hands, oftentimes out of the most meagre piece of scrap. He doesn't talk very much and has a kind heart, which leads some to believe that they can take advantage of him. He manages to laugh this off in his own way because what matters most to him is the act of making and the creation of an object he can be proud of, whether that object is functional or decorative, as simple as table legs or as elaborate as building the most extraordinary of treehouses for his grandson. If I have become a maker, and though my materials are vastly different, I think I owe it to him. He has managed to transmit, in his simple, discreet manner, the joy of manual resourcefulness and the pride and love of a job well done. I am passionate about what I do simply because, in an often confusing world, it is the only thing that genuinely makes any sense."

Using unconventional designer and vintage fabrics, Marie-Michelle makes high-quality, one-of-a-kind handcrafted children's garments. "I have recently started making dolls and stuffed toys crafted entirely from dress cutting remnants, samples, deadstock and roll ends, naturally dyed organic mohair wool and organic cotton muslin, and stuffed with USA-grown and milled organic cotton fibre," she says. "The dolls are meant for play and decorative purposes, and the clothing runs the gamut from Sunday's best to polished semi-casual wear. These creations are a far cry from most 21st century children's dress and toys, and my dearest wish is for them to grow into treasured heirlooms."

"I upcycle all of my cutting remnants and scraps into the making of toys and dolls that have the added benefit of often matching the garments I create. I try to integrate, as much as possible, age-old artisan processes such as natural dyeing, and time-consuming handmade embellishments and embroidery. Nurturing and preserving handcraft and traditional sewing techniques is paramount to my process. My work's most significant trait is perhaps this happy marriage between sustainable resourcefulness and haute couture craft."

With a bachelor of humanities (majoring in French literature with minors in Spanish and theatre studies) and time abroad in Cyprus and France as a translator, Marie-Michelle's adult life has had nomadic phases. "I travel back to France on an annual basis. It is my husband's country, my son's birthplace and the place of origin of some of my ancestors and of my mother tongue. It is also the place where I feel the most at home," she says. Her clothing label, Rastaquouère, keeps her rooted: "It was born out of the necessity of staying sane doing the one thing I enjoy most—creating—regardless and because of life's irregularities, absurdities, amendments, re-routings, estrangements, uprootings and other coarse garden work," she says.

Confessing to an early but temporary aichmophobia (fear of sharp objects) and a frustration at being unable to thread a sewing machine, Marie-Michelle used to avoid the home ec room: "I would've preferred being strapped down to a chair making toothpicks all day in the industrial arts lab with big, brawny boys!" In university, her minor in drama brought her into the world of costume drawing and design. "With the help of my mother-in-law's patience and her 40-year-old cast iron, dependable, clunker of a Singer, my former sewing terror got turned into a passion. All of my learning has been that of a dilettante. I've learned as I've gone along, bungling things, seam ripping, screaming, groaning, hair pulling and generally lacking poise."

Marie-Michelle works from home with a sewing machine that occupies a quarter of the dining room table, with the remaining three quarters

SIEGEL ET STOCKMAN
MADE IN FRANCE

of the table set aside for assembly and embellishment work. "When he isn't jamming with his father on his ukulele, my nine-year-old son sometimes sits with me at the end of the table with his crayons and books when I'm embroidering, and we often joke over invading each other's space, one crayon here or a bobbin of thread there," she says. Fabric cutting happens on the bedroom's maple hardwood floor: "an uncluttered and minimalist space that lends itself well to unfurling great lengths of fabric." Her Stockman-brand mannequins share the landing with the ironing board. "Notions and tools, some of which have been inherited from my mother-in-law and her own grandmother before her, are stored in tin boxes, glass jars and handcrafted walnut boxes. I sometimes

dream about a room of my own, knowing that this will come at the price of losing a piece of this communal camaraderie."

"Because Rastaquouère is basically a one-woman show, I control all aspects of production and am therefore responsible for the garment or the object's journey from start to finish—most of the design, cutting, assembly and finishing, but also embellishment. I find the majority of my materials in the United States and in Europe, which means that the mailman could possibly be my best if fickle friend and that I'm often left waiting several days or weeks between fabric shipments. This in turn can lead to fairly erratic work habits. I rarely work on one project at a time, completing garments and dolls in fits and starts determined by postal deliveries and

stash-busting initiatives. Fabric informs my work in a fundamental way and I make a point of knowing as much as possible about the fabrics I intend to use—where it was grown, where it was made, by whom, how and with what it was dyed. Fabric choice and design choice are often seen as competing variables. I find I'm most successful when the fabric comes first—design then flows naturally from that point onwards, often in starburst. One fabric leads to another, one idea sparks more still."

- **BLOG** *rastacuero.blogspot.ca*
- **SHOP** *rastaquouere.etsy.com*

home sweet home!

TODAY I am filling my

CREATIVE tank

life i design
208 Krieahollo
union
L3R I

Surround yourself
with those who see
thess within

be kind. work hard. stay humble.
smile often. stay loyal. keep honest.
travel when possible. never stop learning.

234

# NICKI TRAIKOS

MARKHAM, ONTARIO, CANADA

Sometimes life takes us in a different direction. For Nicki Traikos, she didn't feel like art was something that she could do for a living, so she enrolled in university—uninspired and unfocused. She left for a year and enrolled in an art course at a local college, and was introduced to everything from sculpting to screen printing to developing photos in a dark room. "I was in heaven," she says.

"But it was time for me to focus on a 'real' job, as I was getting married and we had just bought our first home. So off again I went to university, finished my degree, got a great corporate job with a Fortune 500 company and began to focus on making babies and settling into my grown-up life."

Art and creativity were always in the back of her mind. During her first pregnancy, she took a makeup artistry course. "I had real-life canvases to paint on!" she exclaims. By the time baby number two was on the way, she decided to stay home with her children and work part time as a freelance makeup artist. After a dozen years with a successful career in makeup artistry, she began looking for a change. She pondered her options and imagined what her perfect day might be.

"Then it hit me," she says: "I have always wanted to be an artist! With the support of my

## FOLLOW YOUR DREAMS

"A little over two years ago I was miserable with how I was spending my time (apart from my happy family life)," admits Nicki. "My business made me feel drained, unfulfilled and simply unhappy. With my husband's full support, I took a huge leap of faith, put myself out there, built a rough plan and decided to just dive right in. Succeed or fail, I had to try. I experienced moments of tears, used lots of curse words and felt moments of complete joy. I didn't know the direct route to where I wanted to go, I just knew that I had a dream: To create art and have it touch the people who experience it. To grow a business from it, have it be what I "do" and create a "real job" from it. I still don't know where I'll end up, but I do know that every day my heart is full, I smile and laugh a lot, and I curse a lot less. This creative journey is one that I'll never regret taking. If it's in your blood, you have to just go for it." Nicki created a piece of art for her blog readers that reads "follow your dreams, they know the way". Words to live by.

wonderful husband, I took a six-month sabbatical and went to work on creating a life that I designed." She took courses in Illustrator and Photoshop, designed her website and set up an online shop. "Off I was, drawing, illustrating and typing my way into my new creative life. That was a short two years ago. I am at the height of my creative happiness and can hardly wait to see what the next few years hold!"

After the kids are off to school and the dog is walked, Nicki starts her creative day: "I have a clear head and a hot cup of tea in hand when I head down to my studio. Once in my studio I light a brightly scented, citrusy candle, cue up Maroon 5's latest album on iTunes and look at my never-ending to-do list." She warms up with some calligraphy, doodling or word play. "I let the ink flow, scratch lines into my sketchbook and have a bit of play time. I give myself about 30 minutes to get settled in, then look at my project list and work on the first thing that speaks to me that day."

Nicki makes motivational wall art and home decor items. "Simply hanging a thoughtful wall art print expresses your own creativity and tells a story of who you are. It charges your space with positive energy, pops of inspiration and interest," she says. Typographical and calligraphic sayings are part of a trend, but Nicki embraces this fully: "I love that motivational quotes and hand lettering are a big trend right now. Those two elements are very much a part of me and who I've always been. When I look at my sketchbooks and journals from my teenage years and onwards, I played with verses,

*"What I've learned throughout this creative journey is that when I am most authentic and design from the heart, people respond best to those pieces, and they always sell off the virtual shelf!"*

NICKI TRAIKOS

fancy script writing and sketching images to go along with words. There may be too much of it, but I don't think people are done with that trend quite yet."

Regardless of what may be trendy, in following her passion, Nicki has remained authentic: "Passion isn't something that you can explain—it's what you feel when you are at your happiest. When I was deciding what the next chapter of my life was going to look like, I thought long and hard about how I wanted to spend my days, what I actually wanted to be doing. What difference I could make in other people's lives. What made me really happy and excited. What made my heart sing. I've been able to draw from those feelings, and I decided that I wanted to create art that inspires people and draws out what they are passionate about," she says. "I use simple shapes, colours and words to enhance a personal environment that changes as the person changes. It's who I am. I'm just very lucky that there are others who like what I do."

- WEBSITE/SHOP *lifeidesign.com*
- BLOG *lifeidesign.com/home*
- TWITTER *@lifeidesign*
- INSTAGRAM *@lifeidesign*

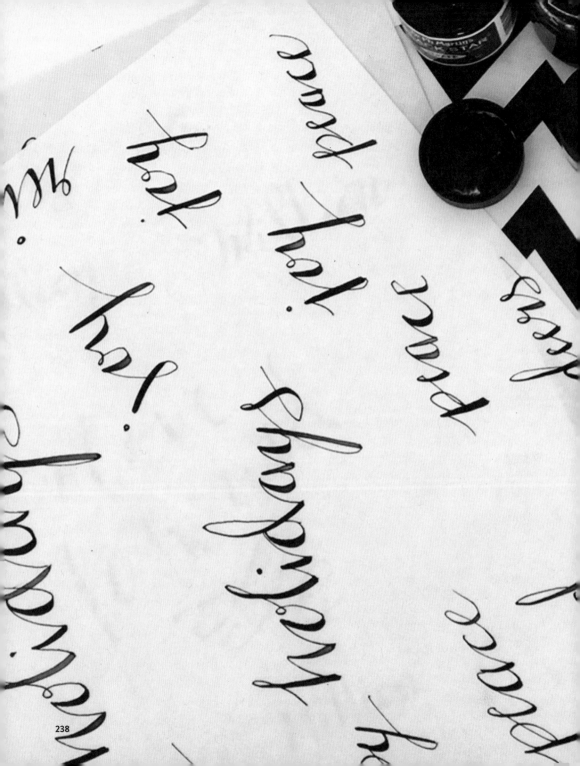

hope tru

hope hope

Grateful

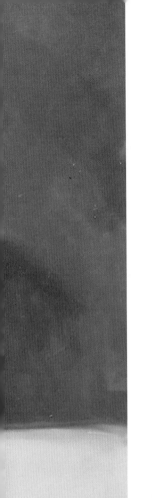

# KIM SMITH

LANCASTER, PENNSYLVANIA, USA

After 25 years of raising her children and owning an advertising and design firm, Kim Smith still feels like she is at the starting line. The pressures of owning a business and parenting are far from over, but she has made the commitment to explore her creativity. "If I don't start to follow my muse now, then when?" she asks. "So, now that my children are 23, 20 and 13, I decided it's time." She gets up at 5 am every day to paint, learn and discover: "Ready. Set. Go."

It takes discipline to start the day so early, but she wakes eager to paint. "I follow my muse and paint whatever inspires me until it's time to get my daughter off to school and myself off to work," she says.

"The most challenging thing is carving out time without feeling guilty that I should be doing something else, that I'm letting other, more important things fall through the cracks." The act of painting inspires her endlessly. "I could wake up in the middle of the night and paint. Anytime. Anywhere. If anything, my challenge is to not let myself run into my studio to paint every chance I get!"

For practicality, she has a tiny studio set up in her home. "It's not terribly charming, and not what I dream of, but it is perfectly suited for me," she says. "It is definitely convenient. I can pick up my paint brush whenever I find a free minute to paint. And my daughter can be doing homework nearby. It's cozy."

Although she has always had a passion for craft, such as art and calligraphy—and these things do relate to her career in advertising and design—painting allows her to create without deadlines or outside pressures and requests. "Pure bliss," she says.

Her medium of choice is oils. The subject matter varies from classic still life subjects to street scenes, but her goal is always to keep the painting fun, free and flowing. "I am waiting for my signature style to find me, although many people tell me I already have one," she says. "A work in progress, yes, that's me for sure." Painting allows her to explore colour, texture and mark-making. "It's always a wonderful surprise—and a little bit sad—when a painting is complete. I love making the world a little more

beautiful, and a little more happy."

"How wonderful would it be to become so busy with creating my artwork that I have no choice but to spend all of my time pursuing my dream of being a 'real' artist?" she muses.

Kim's daily art practice is part of a movement of daily painting and 365 projects, many of which are documented online. "First following and then deciding to join in on the daily painting movement, in my busy, full life, couldn't have been more perfect for me. I can do it in small amounts of time, and in a small space. I can fit it in and make it work."

"I want to be able to inspire others that you don't need to quit your 'real' job or give anything up to squeeze in time to be creative," she says. "That the sky is the limit."

Ready. Set. Go!

- · **WEBSITE** *kimmyerssmith.com*
- · **BLOG** *kimsmithfineart.blogspot.com*
- · **TWITTER** *@kmyerssmithart*
- · **INSTAGRAM** *@kimmyerssmith*

LORI STAHL PHOTOGRAPHY

I must have flowers always & always *Monet*

# KATHRYN COLE

BATESVILLE, ARKANSAS, USA

Kathryn Cole completed a degree in advertising at the University of Texas in Austin, but her heart was in the arts. Upon graduating, she took a job at a flower shop where she daydreamed of someday having her own boutique. She had also discovered metalsmithing, and found a job as an apprentice to a master jeweller. "I learned a lot from him," recalls Kathryn, "and I worked there for a year honing my skills. Then I decided to make the move to Colorado." There, she bought a small bead shop. "I loved owning the bead shop. It was a perfect mix of being creative and working with people and helping them be creative."

"After living in Colorado for 11 years—in a town that claimed they got the most snow in all of Colorado—and with my daughter, who was two at the time, I decided to make the move to Florida to be near family and the ocean. In St. Petersburg I sold my metalwork exclusively online for a couple of years, but missed the daily interactions with people that you get from having a store. I found a wonderful historic area of downtown that had little shops, and after being on a waitlist for some time, I got myself a new shop/studio. I was surrounded by many other artists—painters and designers. It was a wonderfully creative time."

Inspired by her neighbours, Kathryn had the urge to paint and draw again. "A couple of years ago, after some life challenges, I took the leap to learn to be a surface designer and illustrator," she says. "I am so happy now. Each day is different and I love that. I occasionally still do metalwork, but my focus is on surface design and illustrations." She sells original watercolours as well as prints, and sells her

JENNIE THUNELL

surface designs on products such as phone cases and pillows. She has ample experience in person-to-person retail, and what she learned there holds true online: "People love when you create from the heart. I think selling my work informs me as to what people are drawn to."

Using vibrant watercolours, she draws upon her background in floral design to inspire her surface patterns. "I usually have some flowers in my house at all times—fresh cut flowers or orchids or other blooming plants," says Kathryn.

"I love creating in many forms. I love painting, drawing, paper cutting, pattern making, hand lettering and floral designing. There aren't enough hours in the day to do it all, though! Creating brings joy to me. And I hope it brings joy to others, too."

- **WEBSITE** *kathryncoledesign.com*
- **BLOG** *kathryncoledesign.com/blog*
- **SHOP** *butterflyandbloom.com/shop-2*
- **TWITTER** *@kathryncole*
- **INSTAGRAM** *@butterflyandbloom*

# KATE MARSDEN

WALLINGTON, SURREY,
UNITED KINGDOM

Like many of us, Kate Marsden had to put in time at a day job before she was able to make the leap to becoming a full-time creative entrepreneur. Although she studied fashion and textiles in college during the mid-1990s, she worked in a variety of unrelated jobs and ended up spending 15 years at a law firm in London. Her blog and company, Made by Mrs M, began as an outlet for her creativity—at a time when she was desperate for one.

Through her blog and Twitter, she discovered a community of fellow makers and designers. "The blog has become increasingly popular and has taken on a bit of a life of its own!" she says. "I post three times a week and feature my work alongside that of other designers, artists and creatives, as well as regular tutorials, reviews and more." Knowing that there was a

receptive audience made it easier to take the next step toward her own business. After the birth of her son in 2010, the need to pursue her own creativity grew ever stronger. By 2013, she had left her job to pursue her dreams.

"I'm a designer/maker because it's what I always wanted to do," says Kate. "I imagined something like this as a child and I always assumed I'd grow up to be self-employed. The years of working in a non-creative environment taught me a huge amount and have helped to fuel the passion now."

Working from home has been ideal since it allows her to fit work around school and childcare arrangements. She has two rooms: one dedicated to painting, drawing and sewing, and a separate study for computer-based tasks. "Both rooms are very small but I consider myself lucky to have this space so conveniently located, as being at home is particularly important at this time," she says.

Kate focuses on fabric design, and gets her yardage digitally printed in the UK on 100 percent cotton. "My fabrics are aimed at those who sew and craft, as well as interior designers," she explains. "My wider range of complementary products—cushions, lampshades, notebooks, ceramics and other items—are aimed at a wider group of people who are looking for fun but functional, unique designs for their homes and day-to-day lives."

Her current motifs are inspired by architecture: "I take images of striking industrial and modernist buildings and transform them into

bright, simple, repeat patterns." The designs start as a photograph—even a simple snapshot from her phone is adequate. She takes this reference back to the studio where she creates a painting in acrylics or a sketch in pen and ink. "I then scan my original artwork and manipulate the images in Photoshop before creating the patterns."

"It's an old cliché, but pretty much everything inspires me, and I'm sometimes overwhelmed by the quantity of ideas I have. Inspiration often starts with a building, but sometimes it's the juxtaposition of that with florals or a particular colour combination that grabs me."

She sells her work on Etsy and at events such as the Crafty Fox Market and Renegade Craft Fair. "I think that getting out there with your work is vital to prevent stagnation and to get yourself in front of a wider audience. That's the hardest thing for me—getting my work seen—without massive expense or high risks," says Kate.

Being an independent creative company is a lot of work—and a lot of that energy is directed at non-creative activities like selling and marketing and customer service. "Making money is hard," she says. "Getting the average person in the street to understand the time, care and expense involved in creating the item they see is hard." It is a constant process of education, of explaining the costs and efforts involved in the personal manufacture of items that are

unique and not mass produced. "I find it enormously rewarding, though, when people do get it. A high proportion of my customers become repeat customers. This is a great feeling and it also allows me to develop more of a relationship with them, and to learn from their choices and preferences."

"My main motivation is to be able to keep doing this—it's taken me a long time to get here and I don't plan to head back to a corporate environment any time soon!"

- WEBSITE *madebymrsm.co.uk*
- SHOP *etsy.com/shop/madebymrsm*
- TWITTER *@madebymrsm*
- INSTAGRAM *@madebymrsm*

And this is the way to Listen and

become another and you flow
inside their Being
never stopping
to hang on to the door frame
the entrance for security
And you wipe your
words of judgement
upon their mat of trust and
you come to sit among
their joys and concerns and
you Begin to see
and feel their interior
their soul and as the words flow
you find yourself
among the ruins

And you open wide
to feel the space
and this is the way you pause
as you leave at the door
And you thank them
for their welcoming
soul with your eyes
as you listen
to the door gently close
to the outside world.

# KATE BRENNAN HALL

CEDAR FALLS, IOWA, USA

Kate Brennan Hall can remember sneaking little drawings on the endpapers of her siblings' textbooks when she was supposed to be napping. She was just three at the time. "My earliest memories are of drawing—constantly," she says.

She kept up with this passion and attended the Minneapolis College of Art and Design, graduating with a BFA Honours interdisciplinary degree in illustration. Since then she's had a full career: "I've worked for over 25 years as a self-employed illustrator for design firms, ad agencies, magazines and book publishers. My clients have included clients such as Target, the *Atlantic* and Doubleday. My paintings have been exhibited in the US, France and Switzerland. My main focus in the past three years has been the printmaking side of my craft."

"For many years I had my career in a slower gear while raising children and moving around the US. At times I felt a little bit behind my peers but now I can see that I used that time wisely and I've come into this newest chapter of my life full of energy, ideas and excitement. As for motivation, well, I've never lacked it. I was never driven to create from external pressure; it was all internally driven. I'm grateful my parents had very low expectations of me. It let me set my own course for my creative

life—with a lot of help from great teachers and mentors!"

A hallmark of Kate's prints are her blend of written humour and visuals. "I print my writing and designs onto commercial-grade kitchen tea towels. I like to think of my kitchen tea towels as postcards you can wipe your hand on," she says. An added bonus is the giggle (or two) that they elicit. "My writing reflects the general need of connecting with others; spreading love and humour to counteract the sometimes harsh or snarky realities in this modern age of digital disconnection."

"My customers say that my towels are like art for their kitchen. Some even starch and frame them! They are for anyone who wants affordable art that brings a smile to their kitchen,

or their friend's kitchen," Kate says. For her, making an affordable end product is part of the appeal of silkscreening: "I was drawn to illustration and printmaking because you make one image and then create multiples of it so that many people can see the image and therefore maybe it will have more of an impact. It's many versions of one image going out and about and interacting with others."

Kate sells her wares both wholesale and on consignment to shops across the US and Canada. "I've been delighted at the response from my stockists to my designs," says Kate. "There's nothing better than having new retailers reach out to me requesting to carry my goods in their shops." She also sells at art fairs, and via online marketplaces like Supermarket,

Big Cartel, Envelop.eu and Etsy. The diversity of venues and outlets increases her reach as a one-woman operation.

"In this era of handmade it can be challenging to compete with folks who literally have teams of individuals helping them make their 'hand-made' items," says Kate. "Big box stores have gotten very good at carefully packaging their goods to resemble actual handmade goods. Customers can be lulled into thinking that an item is handmade, when in fact it is being made in factories far, far away by hundreds of people. It can be challenging to compete against this model where workers make 50 cents a day."

Working alone has its challenges beyond sim-ply keeping up with demand: "I enjoy being

You're the pick of the Cosmic Litter.

"*Selling my wares becomes like a great conversation that sparks new ideas and gives me new ways of looking at the world and my place in it as an illustrator and print maker.*"

KATE BRENNAN HALL

around people, and the craft life can be a bit solitary. My solution: have a great dog to keep me company and sell at art fairs where I get to meet other artists and my customers. I also enjoy when I can meet my stockists in person (this is getting more difficult as I expand!). I love to see how they have built their creative businesses and to hear what drives their creativity." Interacting with her stockists and customers informs her process and triggers new ideas, but the most rewarding feedback comes from within her own household: "Above all, that my husband and daughters are proud of my work."

Her print studio takes up most of the basement, which she calls "humble but well-loved." It is made up of several areas, including a darkroom, print area, screen cleaning area, ironing area and a photo studio. "My illustration and office area is on the main floor and is filled with the tools of my trade: computer, Wacom tablet, scanner and printer," Kate says. "The walls are full of bulletin boards that have photos of family and friends on them and little scraps of paper that contain hundreds of limericks that my husband pens for me." A string of Christmas lights lends some twinkle year round.

- · **WEBSITE** *katebrennanhall.com*
- · **SHOP** *etsy.com/shop/KateBrennanHall*
- · **TWITTER** *@KateBrennanHall*
- · **INSTAGRAM** *@KateBrennanHall*

PHOTO AT LEFT BY AMY I. RUFFO, ALL OTHERS @NOTTENE

# KIMBERLY ELLEN HALL

### PHILADELPHIA, PENNSYLVANIA, USA

At the centre of Kimberly Hall's naïve drawings and patterns are our relationships with the things around us. Through her Nottene studio, she creates work depicting bottles, shoes, pets, glasses, bicycles and much more. "I love to collect things and I develop relationships and memories with things," she says. "Drawing them has been a way for me to think about the bigger questions I come up against as I live my day-to-day life."

Much of what she creates falls into patterns for fabric companies for their lines, as well as custom illustrations and art prints that she sells direct to consumers: "I really like to do both. In fact I love to have my hands in many projects, so I am always looking for new collaborations and interesting projects to bring my drawings to."

Kimberley says her mother might describe her, even when she was young, as a creative type who doesn't follow the rules. "We have this great recording of her trying to get me to sing 'Mary Had a Little Lamb' for the tape and I just sang the song in silly words and couldn't be persuaded to sing it properly!" she laughs. After growing up in Massachusetts, Kimberley sent time living in New Orleans, Denver, New York and London, working for newspapers,

museums, a fruit stand, fashion brands and even an airplane parts office, before opening her studio in Philadelphia.

The disregard for the rules that she showed as a child suits her illustration style well: "I know my customers—the people my work attracts— are looking for that special touch of a hand-drawn line, something real and messy and not necessarily perfect to remind them about what the real world is like: messy and imperfect!" she explains. "My line is clean but wavering, my colours are soft but bold. I like to tug on the balance or symmetry of a piece so that it's just a bit... off."

"Drawing is a technique that I have slowly honed over the years. It just seemed like I always thought of myself as kind of bad sketcher and then suddenly I could draw, but really it

was just years of doing it anyway, even though I wasn't very good at it. That makes me love it even more." She speaks fondly of a Maira Kalman quote about a painting being truer than a photograph: "I think that is true for a drawing, as well."

Kimberley's Nottene studio is on the top floor of a row house in Philadelphia. "We set up a white table near the window for computer work and still life photoshoots, plus a 'messy table' in the centre of the room where any of us, kids included, can work freely," she says. "I also tend to read and use books in our TV room/library. It's the coziest space in winter and full of my favourite thrift store books."

Living and working in Philadelphia has been a major part of developing both her business and her own work. "I am thoroughly enam-

oured with the city," she says.

One of her early projects involved selling vintage clothes as illustrations only. "Although it was an interesting concept, it just didn't sell," she recalls. "I realized that people wouldn't invest in a drawing of something they didn't already have a relationship with. That was just a new dress. What they wanted commemorated were items they kept stashed in their closet or something their baby had outgrown but they cherished."

- **WEBSITE** *nottene.net*
- **BLOG** *nottene.net/notes*
- **SHOP** *nottene.net/shop*
- **TWITTER** *@nottene_kim*
- **INSTAGRAM** *@nottene*

# KRIS BOSSENBROEK-FOUSERT

ERMELO, GELDERLAND, THE NETHERLANDS

While reading *The Artist's Way* by Julia Cameron, Kris Bossen-broek-Fousert made a decision: to create, make happy things and sell them. The attic in her house was free, so she claimed that as her space. She was 37 at the time, and her husband was building a home office for his business. "I used to work for him, doing the administration and bookkeeping, but didn't like it very much," she confesses. "It was my chance to begin my own business."

She designed a set of collaged cards, printed them and opened a web shop, called By Kris. "Within a year, a wholesaler wanted to distribute my cards, and in 2011 they were sold in gift stores and bookshops in the Netherlands. I was over the moon," she says.

"Upstairs in the attic I have my atelier: it is one explosion of colour. I enjoy working in a big mess with all the stuff that I need. When I start a new project I clean up all the chaos and start all over again. I have a record player and love to listen to old records for inspiration and to get in a good mood." When she is getting down to business and filling orders, she does this from her office. "I have my storage and web shop and computer, and it is where I spend a lot of time. They are pretty neat surroundings."

Her illustrations, paintings and collages use mixed-media techniques incorporating print ephemera and found imagery. She is inspired by thrift stores, old magazines and vintage fashion. "The By Kris designs are very

recognizable for their particular collage style and their retro feeling," says Kris. "My designs are always colourful and almost chaotic. They bring a smile to people's faces." Her process is immediate and instinctual: "I usually don't think too long, I just begin." It is a fun cycle of collecting, cutting, drawing, painting, writing, gluing, scanning and collaging.

In 2011, Kris organized a round robin notebook project. Participants within groups filled Moleskine sketchbooks with collages, recipes, drawings, writing and whatever their hearts desired. She created an online forum and produced three issues of *Robin Magazine* to share the work. "I love to stimulate people to discover their creative skills," she says. "*Robin Magazine* was one of the reasons why I got a freelance job at a real publisher, and now I am a creative editor and stylist for a Dutch women's magazine. I am still surprised and thankful how my life has gone the past few years. Just by doing what I like, taking opportunities and believing in myself."

Self-confidence and good intuition are helpful attributes for artists in business; they can take you a long way. "I don't make a detailed plan, I just start and then the magic will happen. Or not, and then the challenge is to puzzle it out until it's right," says Kris. "I think I am at my best when I am creating. It feels like a gift that I need to use to be the real me."

- **WEBSITE** *bykris.nl*
- **INSTAGRAM** *@bykris*

## WHAT IF?

"What if someday nothing comes out from my fingers?" Kris has wondered. "What if my inspiration is empty?" We have all experienced those days of struggle. Her advice? "I have learned that sometimes you have to let it go. Doing something else, like crocheting or writing or having fun with friends, can help you get over it."

*"My inspiration comes from things that I see. Or hear. Or dream. Or from walking in a thrift store, or reading an old magazine."*

KRIS BOSSENBROEK-
FOUSERT

# KIRRILY WALKER

HAZELBROOK, NEW SOUTH WALES, AUSTRALIA

Sometimes listening to customers can allow a maker to find a niche. Kirrily Walker opened her Needle vs Thread store on Etsy in 2006 after asking for a sewing machine for Christmas the year before. She was making bags mostly out of vinyl, but using some leather as well. Over the years, customers asked her whether her bags were leather or vinyl, hoping it was the latter. "This led me to the decision to eliminate all leather (and wool and silk) and make Needle vs Thread 100 percent vegan," she says. "The customer response has been overwhelmingly positive, and it proves the value in listening to your customers."

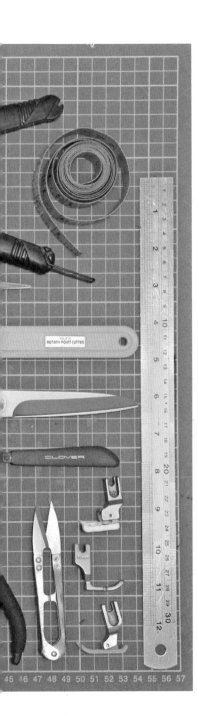

Prior to getting a sewing machine—which she wanted so that she could alter her own clothes—sewing was not of particular interest to her. "I was born with brittle bones, grew up in a small country town and got my first wheelchair around the age of 10," Kirrily says. "Due to location and obvious mobility issues, I spent much of my childhood indoors, and my mother kept me busy experimenting with various crafts. None of them really struck a chord with me—including sewing!" Instead, she studied graphic design at university.

Selling online has been a natural fit for Kirrily, and Needle vs Thread has drawn customers from all over the world. But selling at markets presented challenges for Kirrily that most vendors don't face: "As a wheelchair user, working at the markets probably wasn't the ideal or most obvious choice, as there are challenges with access at many venues, but I've found plenty of markets that work for me and now

trade one or two days a week. Markets are a fantastic way to sell, as you interact directly with customers and learn why they do (and don't) buy things, what they love and what they would like you to add to your range. The feedback is invaluable."

She also appreciates the community around these markets. "I like to work in a bubble, without distraction, so I often feel like I don't fit the gregarious artist stereotype. But as a maker who sells at markets, I have a strong community of fellow stall holders—both those who make their products and those who don't—and customers. They may not all be creative, but we spend lots of time talking about sewing, fashion, design and business, and it is nice to have a variety of viewpoints on all of this."

She has created a large studio in one room of her house, but as a renter she can't make any permanent changes. Instead, she has made use of creative thinking, plus lots of racks, shelves and pegboard. "Over the past few years I've amassed an array of tools that make my job possible," she says. "I have a few different sewing machines, an ironing press and a really good iron, a rivet press, an electric fabric cutter, rotary cutters, specialty scissors, punches, a butane torch and a series of other tools. Everything is set up within easy reach for maximum efficiency. This works well for me—it's accessible, there's no commute, I can work whenever and however late I need to and get to spend all day with my dogs!"

Among her work, she is most proud of her new line of backpacks: "They represent the culmination of all of my sewing and design skills. The process of making them is much different from and more difficult than all my other bags, and they are something I wouldn't have been able to make a year or two ago."

Kirrily describes herself as competitive by nature, and that competitiveness motivates her. "I keep detailed records about how many bags I sell, and each month or quarter or year or market I want to sell more than the last. This motivates me to make more bags so I can try to beat my own record! Selling at markets every weekend means I always need to have a certain amount of stock, so I have a weekly deadline that helps ensure I keep making."

Though she is proud of the quality of her craftsmanship, craftsmanship is not necessarily what customers notice first: "I find my work sitting in a funny spot these days where the handmade aspect is not necessarily front and centre. Customers often initially think my work is factory-produced, and that secretly pleases me because I equate it with the perception of professionalism."

- **WEBSITE** *needlevsthread.com*
- **SHOP** *etsy.com/shop/needlevsthread*

*"I'm a maker because I don't like to sit still. I don't like idle hands and I don't believe in manicured nails! I like details and giving attention to them. I like fabric and shiny metal hardware, and the fact that I have developed the skills to turn these things into a functional and beautiful object, and that not everyone can do that."*

KIRRILY WALKER

# MIRIAM HAEFELE

STUTTGART,
BADEN-WÜRTTEMBERG, GERMANY

"The first step is collecting ideas." This is wise advice from Stuttgart-based artist Miriam Haefele. It is even more apt when one discovers that she is trained as a librarian. "I've always been interested in art and illustration," says Miriam. "In 2011, I took a sabbatical and spent some creative months in London, drawing, taking pictures and learning all sorts of printing techniques. Back home, I turned my day job into part time and started my own creative business."

"As a librarian I mostly worked using my brain. As a maker I can use my brain, my heart and my hands," she explains. "Creating makes me feel alive." With a repertoire comprising illustration, hand-lettering, photography and printmaking, Miriam prefers to create things she deems "useful," such as greeting cards, hand-printed clothes and bags, and rubber stamps. "I use all sorts of materials—paper old and new, fabric, old dishes, etc.—but my all-time favourite is paper." Here again, her background in library science is apparent. "I create for like-minded people and, admittedly, for myself."

As part of her creative process, she fills her sketchbooks with drawings and notes of things that attract her attention or come to mind. She supplements her collection of ideas with photographs. "Association and coincidence are also part of the process. I've often found playing around and making mistakes helpful and rather great fun," she says.

Miriam does not intentionally follow any current trends in style, but recognizes that hand-made, upcycled and eco-friendly materials are certainly of the moment. "I sell my work online on DaWanda—the equivalent of Etsy in Ger-

many—and I'm about to open my Etsy shop. I also sell to some brick-and-mortar stores and occasionally set up a stall at craft markets."

"Selling my craft shows me that people react to my work—in all sorts of ways. Selling at craft markets is the best way to get in touch with people. Some visitors look at the whole stall very closely. Some people like to touch my wares and feel the material they're made of. Some people even stroke my fox illustration very gently (which is very touching for me!). People tell me about their associations with my creations. Some people just look at everything very closely and smile to themselves or even laugh out loud because they find my illustrations and texts, most of which are in German, so funny. All this is very rewarding for me. I also like when people tell me that they don't like my work and why. People have different views and tastes, and I like to hear about that. Selling my wares does inform my creativity. Many new products have resulted from interactions with my customers. For example when people told me they liked one of my designs and would love to buy it in the form of another product. My hand-lettering is another example: I had never planned to do that. But people kept

"*What I love about being creative is that there are no limits to your imagination. You can think it up? Then you can make it! Sometimes you can even take yourself by surprise!*"

MIRIAM HAEFELE

telling me how much they adored my hand-written price tags, so I included hand-lettering into my repertoire."

But making things by hand and offering them for sale can be limiting: "Dealing with orders can prevent you from creating new work—it's a challenge to keep the two in balance. Setting prices is also a difficult task." It's also demanding to keep up with production, Miriam says: "I have reached a point where I think I'll have to shift the emphasis. Much as I love the hand-made aspect of creativity I need to concentrate more on designing and let a printer do the production." She is not willing to let go of hand-made entirely, though. "At least a small part of my products will always be handmade by me."

Miriam's advice for staying inspired and motivated in one's craft? "In my opinion, staying curious is the key. Everything around me can be inspiring. If anything becomes a routine I find it helpful to imagine being a tourist or newbie: look at things as if you'd never seen them before!" She recommends travelling as a tool for making new experiences. "Awareness, observation, association and a few drops of coincidence is a recipe I can recommend," Miriam says. "Be open and ideas will come to you."

- **WEBSITE** *mimifaktur.de*
- **BLOG** *blog.mimifaktur.de*
- **SHOP** *de.dawanda.com/shop/mimifaktur*

"*Birds fly, fish swim and I make things. It's simply what I do, and have done since I was a young child; it feels as natural and necessary as eating and sleeping.*"

NADIA HASSAN

# NADIA HASSAN

GREENSBORO,
NORTH CAROLINA, USA

"I love my studio," declares Nadia Hassan from her cheerful and bright creative space in her home where she lives with her partner, his two children and a grey cat named Toby.

"It's a sanctuary. But it's also a battleground for the minimalist and the magpie perched on my shoulders (my personal version of the angel/devil metaphor, I guess). One is allergic to clutter and mess, and the other is a compulsive collector—beads, buttons, bottle caps, paint chips from hardware stores. So far, each has won a few battles, but neither has won the war."

"I've filled it with an abundance of orange and aqua, my two very favourites from a long list of favourite colours. I have a 'proper' desk setup, but more often than not I create while standing over my work table, sitting on the floor or lounging on the couch with my laptop—habits that were no doubt formed during my work-wherever-space-allows days." It has been said that peering into an artist's studio is akin to peering into the mind of the artist,

DANA DILLEHUNT

though Nadia disputes this: "Visitors often re-mark how organized the space is. I just chuckle and tell them that I'm overcompensating for a chaotic mind!"

If Nadia were to write her autobiography, she would title it "My Life as a Spork." It's a curi-ous title, for sure. What does it mean? "Being almost one thing but not quite another is a common thread throughout my life," she ex-plains. "I was a half-Lebanese girl with a decid-edly foreign name growing up in rural North Carolina. So from an early age, I learned to be comfortable with not fitting neatly into any one category."

Not fitting into a predefined box is, overall, a benefit to her outlook on life, and her career, says Nadia: "Fortunately, my early experience with being something of an anomaly taught

me that it could be an asset rather than a burden. Though sometimes I still feel insecure about my hybrid status as an artist/designer, I realize that I'm far from the only one who straddles, blurs or outright ignores the line between artist and designer."

"I make artwork—sometimes as a standalone piece, sometimes as a repeating pattern—for bolt fabric, wall art, stationery, apparel, home decor, gifts and accessories, and pretty much anything else that will sit still. I work digitally, incorporating handmade textures and illustrations to add depth and interest to my finished pieces. My work is for anyone who likes pattern and colour. Because it tends to be bright and happy, it often shows up in nurseries and kids rooms, on baby clothes, on phone cases and other accessories, and in quilts, bags and other sewn goods."

Not formally trained in surface design, Nadia credits the Internet and services like print-on-demand fabric supplier Spoonflower for opening the door for her to the industry. "We are graphic designers, illustrators and fine artists who are able to break into an industry that, until recently, was off-limits to outsiders," she says. Through a tight-knit online community, Nadia finds resources, support and even feedback on her work. "We celebrate our successes and support each other when we face obstacles. There's no official group, and different people are more active on different platforms, but it's really wonderful to feel a sense of closeness and community with so many others, despite never having met most of them in person!"

Nadia works with a licensing agent to help get her work out to market. "Now that I'm working with a licensing agent, I feel a bit like I'm back in school; I have so much to learn!" she says. "My whole perspective about what's possible to achieve has changed, and I'm still wrapping my head around it."

Her style is evolving as she learns the ropes of the industry, but her designs usually include bold graphics, clean lines and cheerful colours. "I enjoy experimenting with abstraction, interlocking shapes, and the delicate balance between positive and negative space," Nadia explains. She is shifting from solely working digitally to incorporating more handmade elements through calligraphy, lettering, watercolour and collage. "I enjoy being a style chameleon, though it goes against the conventional wisdom that you need a signature style to have a successful career as an artist. I want to continue exploring different styles and subject matter, and after enough time I should be able to pick out unmistakable trends within my work. I don't think I've reached that point yet, but I'm not necessarily in a hurry; I tend to relish the journey more than the destination."

- **WEBSITE** *nadiahassan.com*
- **BLOG** *patternoftheweek.tumblr.com*
- **SHOP** *synaestheticstudio.etsy.com*
- **TWITTER** *@modmagpie*
- **INSTAGRAM** *@modmagpie*

# RACHELLE CHUANG

ALISO VIEJO, CALIFORNIA, USA

Rachelle Chuang's calling often seems to be as much about teaching her craft as the craft itself. "Though I have had my work in several exhibitions and published in books, my career highlights are every day in the classroom," she says. "When students achieve excellence, discover their own creativity and push themselves to new heights, these are highlights I see every day. If I've inspired just one student to go further than they ever thought they would, then it's all worth it."

Her teaching is divided between the arts departments of Biola University, Chapman University, Irvine Valley College and Laguna College of Art and Design. Most of her own work, which consists of complex and colourful letterpress prints, springs from a desire to teach: "My prints are created primarily for an educational context," she says. "My latest print series showcases experimental typography using antique wood type and the found shapes that are created through overprinting and overlapping. The series also functions as educational samples about the qualities of ink and paper, and colour theory."

But her works do not look like lessons; instead they are colourful, playful, typographic and experimental. "Hopefully they communicate my immense love for both paper and print," she says. "I also keep my work simple and beautiful. My prints are joyfully colourful and transmit the timeless qualities of pure ink on paper and the tactile qualities of traditional letterpress."

This experimental, creative approach to typography is something she traces back to her childhood: "I've loved typographic objects my whole life, from the blocks I had as a kid to Letraset rub-down letters and now letterpress. Typographic objects and systems have been a constant fascination. I've been fortunate to have many people believe in me at every stage of my life, and one of the reasons I'm a teacher is to pay it forward. It only takes one person to change someone's entire trajectory."

In addition to the printmaking studio at Biola University, she also has a small studio space in her garage. Both places have a Vandercook 4 press, and she shuttles her wood type collection between them. "I have to store my wood type in large pizza boxes so they are transportable between both spaces," she says, "but I sure wish I had room for permanent storage!" Her garage workshop has two walls full of letterpress examples. One is covered with prints she has collected over the years from Hatch Show Print, Church of Type, Hamilton Wood Type and Printing Museum, International Museum and many printmakers. The other wall holds her various typographic experiments and ephemera she has printed. "This allows me to see my colour schemes and ink properties in one fell swoop."

Rachelle's preference for wood type comes from how it facilitates teaching. "I like to use real wood type because working with letters as objects imparts typographic principles in ways that can't be learned on a computer," she explains. "Kerning, leading, balance, proportion, composition, alignment and working within natural limitations are all part of the process. Because I love design history, introducing students to historic letterpress really makes them light up and discover an old process and its beauty. For my own work, I use letterpress in ways conducive to my objectives. The overlapping type series was designed to show properties of ink and paper, such as CMYK, analogous colours, found shapes that occur when overlapping, symmetry and other

*"I'll tell you what motivates me: the truth that it's not all about me. My self-image and confidence does not rise and fall on my ego, fame or accomplishments. What motivates me is that I am part of this great big stream of incredible creativity. When I look at all the great things on Pinterest, it motivates me to keep working to get to the next level out of aspiration and gratitude, not from a place of obsessive envy or jealousy."*

RACHELLE CHUANG

considerations. Wood type letters are selected and locked up on either of my Vandercook 4 presses, ink is mixed and applied to the rollers and away we go!"

"Our lives are just so full and so crowded," she says. "If you want to pursue something well, then you have to choose to make space for it. I never let cultural expectations drag me along, so there are many things I choose not to do, like being on a million social media spaces. I intentionally build in lots of margin and buffer space so I can engage in creative play and production at my own pace. Believe me, I have a very full life teaching at four universities, but I easily say no to many good things to make way for what I believe are the best things—real relationships, the rest of the body and soul, creative activity, holistic health."

"Making is essential to who we are as humans," she continues. "As a Christian, I believe that we are made in the image of God and have the ability to create as a result. Whether you agree with this or not, I think we can all agree that making is such a fundamental part of the full breadth of the human experience. Making is basically creating. Whether it is cooking food, composing music, choreographing a dance, sculpting, painting, collaging, printing or even designing a rocket, the makers are using their ingenuity, resourcefulness and creativity as part of the process."

• **WEBSITE** *saatchiart.com/colorblissstudio*

*"Certainly inspiration comes and goes, but I love approaching it Elizabeth Gilbert-style: do the work. If I get in and start working, pretty soon I can't help but feel inspired, no matter how I felt to begin with. It's a beautiful thing."*

STEPHANIE
SEAL BROWN

# STEPHANIE SEAL BROWN

LOUISVILLE, KENTUCKY, USA

"Creating with my hands has always been an ideal offset to an over-active mind: embroidery and philosophy, quilting and calculus, sewing and studying," says Stephanie Seal Brown. With weaving, Stephanie has found her calling, in creating linen tape trim for the interior design industry that is used on drapery, upholstery and soft goods such as throw pillows. It is work that balances precision with luxurious simplicity.

"I am a handloom weaver working with tradi-tional, human-powered equipment all the way through production up until the last moment when a burst of steam helps to set the weave," she says. "Working slowly with each individual linen yarn at a time, I am able to imbue my work with a strong sense of identity and pur-pose." She sees herself as part of movement to redefine American manufacturing, to bring it home, and to make it personal. "We are looking at our skills, resources and passions, and cre-ating unique products based on what we offer better than anyone else."

"I see makers as a key bridge piece in the American manufacturing story. A strong manufacturing economy is built on finding the best expression of available resources in a

geographic area, and as makers we are taking the best of our resources and applying incredible levels of ingenuity, creating new ways to connect with product and how we use products in our daily lives."

Louisville, Kentucky, is an excellent community for makers and artists. Her bright and airy studio is inside an historic worsted mill along the L&N (Louisville and Nashville) Railroad: "I am surrounded by a number of professional artisans: glass artists, sculptors, painters, a milliner and photographers. It is incredibly helpful to have folks from all different disciplines facing many of the same issues and able to talk through possible solutions—not to mention the inspiration of seeing so many different types of work evolving all around you."

Her linen tapes are beautiful and, most often, striped. "Stripes. I love stripes," Stephanie says. "My goal in design is to distill expression into its simplest form—to just before it becomes nonexistent—and that is where you find its most effective face. I feel that stripes in the simplest construction of cloth represent this simplicity at its most elegant."

"Simplicity in anything demands the highest quality of raw materials. I work with European linen yarns out of a Swedish dye house that are not only beautiful in sheen and colour, but are held up to very high environmental standards in production."

Although her work appears simple, it does not belie the considerable skill or dedication required to execute it. Stephanie has also cre-

ated fine and more complex designs but was surprised by the reaction from customers. "I learned the importance of keeping the work exquisite but relatable. I learned by watching people's faces that the finer my work became—the finer the yarns that I worked with, the more intricate the patterns—the harder it was for them to relate to it as handwoven. When I showed work that allowed folks to see the nuance and character of the handwoven structure more readily, they grasped it and valued it more."

Stephanie recognizes that the perceived value of the work is a real challenge in the realm of handmade: "Every maker I know has this incredible set of skills and is looking at a seemingly limitless, yet often inaccessible, market out there. To me, the key is chasing down one's own unique rabbit hole of inspiration and passion and developing a product line that best expresses it. This requires a challenging vote of confidence in one's own vision that is an interesting intersection of the artist (exposure) and manufacturer (scaled market prediction). Once that vote is cast, the unique path to market has to be worked out for each individual maker. There is no formula, and this is hard. And incredibly rewarding."

- **WEBSITE** *stephaniesealbrown.com*

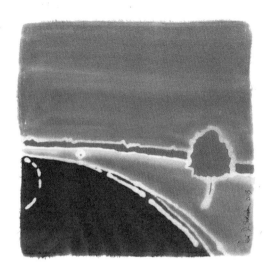

# RENÉ SHOEMAKER

ATHENS, GEORGIA, USA

"I wake up in the morning ready to create; I am driven by an internal engine to work," René Shoemaker says from her home in the woods of Northeast Georgia. "I arise filled with anticipation for what will be created that day, and with a desire to see the morning sky. I have waited for many years to act on this sense of purpose, and I have used those years to build a skill set that enables me to do what I am passionate about."

A fibre artist trained at the University of Georgia, she stayed on at the university following graduation when offered a job in the library. She continued to take classes and discovered painting on silk: "As soon as I tried it, I fell in love with the immediacy of the colour and design work in surface design. I never stopped creating, although raising two children, as well as living for a while in a house without electricity, limited the time I had to create." She retired from the university a few years ago. "Now I am happy to have a dedicated studio (with water

 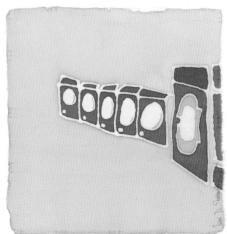

and electricity!) and the time to dedicate to my craft," she says. "I treasure this opportunity to create art full time."

Her studio is situated behind her homemade house. "My husband and I built our house by hand from material found on the land or re-purposed from other buildings," says René. "We built the studio a few years later, and it is tiny—15 feet by 12 feet—but it has good light, large windows and a great work table. Because there are no other houses around us, it is very quiet, and I am able to commune with nature as I work. And the sunsets are exquisite."

The vibrant hues of these sunsets find their way into her work: silks dyed with strong, confident colours. "I paint abstract, impressionistic renderings of the built environment," René says, describing her work. "My paintings enliven a space with colour and force; they are made for homes and public spaces. The silk

takes colour beautifully; the silk and the colour bond and become one through the process of creating the work. The silk has texture and dimensionality, yet is light and airy."

Her works can be quite large and are usually installed hanging from the ceiling, almost like a mobile. "When you walk under them, you can often see them billow, pivot and shift in response to your movement," she says. "I often work with architectural images, reducing them to basic shapes and highlighting character and detail. I am seeking poetry and harmony, but visually, using line and colour. The paintings resonate with viewers, evoking a sense of recognition. Many locations have a soul of their own that I try to represent through colours and line."

From her location sketches, she further simplifies the design almost to the point of abstraction: "This is when I am happiest—when a de-

sign is broken down into its elemental forms." Once the design is transferred to the silk, she stretches the materials so that she can draw on the resist lines. These remain white in the finished painting, René explains: "The resist keeps one colour dye from merging with its neighbour." Next, she mixes her dyes ("I rarely use a colour right out of the dye pot) and applies the dye by brush, working carefully and quickly before it begins to dry. "I am ecstatic when the colour goes down. Colour is the guiding force in my paintings, the essence of the design." The following day, she rolls the silk in newsprint and steams it to set the dye. Following a wash and iron, the artwork is completed.

René loves to travel, sketching as she goes. "I do my best to discover new places that spark my curiosity. I begin the process by sketching on site. I love to look at the space in public areas, the relationship between buildings, and the small architectural details that give a building character," she says. These in situ sketches resulted in her first international exhibition. "Most recently, a café in Paris hosted an exhibition of a series of prints I made, based on café tables I sketched while travelling in France. The prints were inspired by quiet moments while travelling, by taking in a place, experiencing that place fully, then working in the style that feels most natural to me."

New places can teach us new ways of doing things, but travel also exercises our ability to observe. "Creativity keeps my eyes sharp and my focus clear," says René. "But even at home I pick up interesting patterns of light and shadow—shapes and their relationships stand out to me, and negative space is particularly vivid. I love to watch how people use a space, how they interact with it and are shaped by it, and develop a relationship with it in a way they may not

even be aware of. In my designs I try to sim-plify, simplify, simplify, almost to the point of abstraction, and always to pull out a detail that might otherwise be lost in the bigger picture."

"I have a recognizable style: a creative use of colour and simplified shapes, along with strong line drawing on silk," she says. "Late-ly I have been translating this style into other techniques and materials. I've been creating linoleum prints, using similar line and compo-sition, and the response has been wonderful. For me, the prints on paper and the paintings on silk share the same aesthetic, although to others they may seem very different. The paper I print on is 100 percent cotton, so in a way we could call it fibre design also!"

- **WEBSITE/BLOG** *reneshoemaker.com*
- **INSTAGRAM** *@coffeecupress*

## ON BEING IN BUSINESS FOR ONESELF

Being in business for oneself is challenging because the income is never guaranteed. "As a full-time artist I have to think strategically about how to pay the bills," says René. "This is a new skill set I am just beginning to learn. Artists are able to define success for themselves, but they need to know how to promote their own work—it's not the time to be shy! Learning how to contact the media for press, locate exhibition spaces, create a following on social media and in the real-world com-munity, and enhance the collectors' experience is a job in itself. Currently I spend three to five days a week in the studio and another two days a week contacting people, arranging face-to-face meetings, researching new supplies and where to find them, and spending inspiration time at museums and other art centres."

# MITHRA BALLESTEROS

MEQUON, WASHINGTON, USA

"Self-doubt is an albatross around the neck of anyone who makes things and puts them into the world," asserts Mithra Ballesteros, a collector, curator, stylist and photographer. "Not a day goes by when I don't chant to myself: 'Just keep swimming. Just keep swimming.' Of course the reward is the speed with which the days fly by. I am extremely happy in my work."

Mithra creates collections of objects and art. "My collections are made of discarded items and things that society deems not very valuable," she says. "After creating a collection, I write about it on my blog. Each collection is absolutely one of a kind. It bridges the past and the present, sparks conversation, inspires exploration. People who like my collections are drawn to the vibration of history coming off of them." Impeccably styled and photographed, the objects are sold as a complete set—the owner purchasing not only the objects, but the story and style of those things juxtaposed with each other.

Gathered not only for their aesthetic value, the objects have deeper resonance: "I'm not even sure if I am a maker, necessarily. I feel I'm more of a caretaker. For all of my life, I have believed that objects have souls. They have an essence. I just help others to see their essence,

RENN KUHNEN

309

*"I am motivated by stubbornness. I believe that every house could benefit from collections like mine that link the past and the present."*

MITHRA BALLESTEROS

too." Mithra believes that consumers need to be thoughtful about the items they surround themselves with. "This consciousness has happened in the food industry but it needs to happen in the home, too. People need to consider the hidden costs when they shop at Pottery Barn or HomeGoods."

"I hope my collections inspire people to recycle and repurpose. I hope people will turn away from the faux-aged or the mass-produced and instead seek out things with that intangible quality of aging."

Her attraction to and reverence of objects is rooted in her unique family history. "I was born in Iran to an American mother and an Iranian father," she explains. "I am amazed that my mother left her Midwestern family and moved to Iran to start a family. I am equally amazed that, years later, my father decided to move us back to the US. Both of my parents experienced the process of leaving possessions behind to make a new life across the ocean. For that reason, what little they had was highly valued and very sentimental."

"My parents taught me to work hard in order that my children could be better off than me. Now that I am nearly done raising four sons, I feel like I've earned the right to follow a more creative, less conventional path. I have saved enough money to experiment a little and I'm not so worried about the future. It is very liberating to be over 50 and taking risks."

Mithra revels in the joyful process of gathering: "I search high and low—at junk shops and

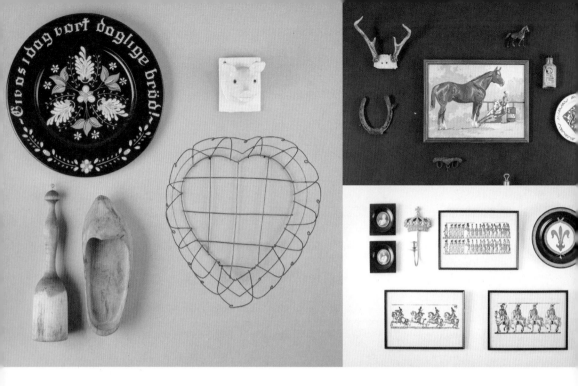

auctions and garage sales—and never fail to find an element with potential. When I am on the hunt, I relax and zone out. By deliberately blurring my vision a little, it makes it easier to see the true essence of an object. When I bring the object home, I live with it for a while, and mix it with different, often disparate things. When a collection begins to come together, I make a space for it somewhere in my house."

Reclaiming the family's basement as her own, she keeps her studio lights permanently set up and at the ready. "It actually was my kids' playroom for 20 years and now it's where I play—though one can't imagine the guilt when I packed up their drum sets and painted over their graffiti art," she says. Each wall is painted a different colour for use as photographic backdrops. "I have one son left at home and he

has a tiny corner with an old tube TV. But he doesn't complain. He likes wandering through the space, fingering all my treasures."

It can take months for a collection to come together and be ready for a photograph. "The best part is finding the final piece," says Mithra. "I always know it when I see it because we lock eyes and I get goose bumps. And of course, looking at it through the camera lens is the final confirmation that it is finished."

She sells her work in her online shop, Finder Not Keeper, as well as on the independent maker site Scoutmob and a small, physical pop-up shop. "For me, the challenge has been to explain what I'm selling," she says. "On a purely technical basis, I'm not even sure what keywords to use so people can find me. For the most part, I let my images do the talking.

This approach is only recently possible thanks to the explosion of Pinterest and Instagram. Today, creating great pinnable images is just as valid a marketing plan as incorporating strong SEO."

Motivated by the process of and opportunity for creative expression, Mithra admits that it is a labour of love. "At the same time, I've learned so much in the process of selling," she says. "Communication is key. Good writing coupled with good photography is the best way to get past the computer screen—and into the imagination of the user."

- **WEBSITE/SHOP** *findernotkeeper.com*
- **BLOG** *thebubblejoy.com*
- **TWITTER** *@findernotkeeper*
- **INSTAGRAM** *@findernotkeeper*

# SARAH AMIJO

JAKARTA, INDONESIA

"I have drawn hundreds of illustrations, but I still feel a great euphoria when I finish colouring any project," says Sarah Amijo. The joy she gets from her illustrations is felt by her customers, too—very often, in fact, she is drawing darling creatures that are representative of the customers themselves. "I create animal character illustrations. My clients pick an animal from the Friendly Creatures Collection that I have created and personalize their chosen creatures with custom accessories." The individualized characters are digitally printed on a product of the client's choosing: phone cases, canvasses, greeting cards or journals.

After many rounds of sketches and doodles, the illustration is finished with washes of watercolour and details using colour pencils, thin markers or brushes. "Colouring feels a lot like giving an inanimate paper a breath of life, with my brush slowly filling the life force of the character, stroke-by-stroke" she says. Sarah prefers to stay within an earthy, delicate range of colours for an overall rustic and vintage feel. "All my creatures are rounded, chubby and huggable," she says, smiling.

The personalization that Sarah offers is part of what makes her approach unique: "I feel no greater joy than when a customer picks one of my illustrations as a representation of

themselves or gift it to their loved ones. These feelings drive me to create more adorable character illustrations."

Sarah works day and night from her studio apartment in Jakarta: "I do most of my sketches and outlining at night, and draw them the next morning. Natural sunlight not only lets me colour more accurately, but it also gives me a much-needed mood boost to colour wholeheartedly."

Dealing with cuteness and colours is worlds away from her first career in accounting, a profession she initially pursued for its higher salary and job opportunities. "I worked as an accountant for about a year, before finally realizing that accounting was not my passion," she says. With fond regard for her high school art class, she realized that she could do much more with drawing. "I applied to an art graduate program. It was a big gamble for me as the chance to get accepted without an undergraduate degree in art was very slim." With what she credits as a "divine blessing," Sarah was accepted into the program and learned a great deal. "I was fortunate to learn under inspiring mentors in the program who pushed and guided me to become an artist, as I am right now."

Known as the "Queen of Cute," Sarah rejected this title at first, disliking the stereotype. Eventually, though, she understood her strengths, and with guidance from her college mentors, she has embraced a style that has become her signature.

The income for entrepreneurial artists in Indonesia is relatively low compared to traditional fields, but Sarah asserts that the opportunity

to do what she loves every day is valuable. She gives special thanks to her loving and supporting husband. "I don't feel burdened working long hours while doing what I am passionate about," she says.

Pricing her work is a delicate matter: "Art is very subjective. My true loyal fans will spend money on it, but those who have a different vision might try to bargain or even compare my work to other artists who offer lower prices."

To balance her product offerings, she released her first line of printed stationery under her Big Bear and Bird brand. "I was initially a bit worried, as it was the first time I was printing and stocking a large quantity of non-personalized stationery products," she explains. "Up until that moment, I had only been selling custom-ordered personalized stationery prod-

ucts." Fortunately, the launch was encouraging and it has given her confidence to produce more stationery products in the future. "I'm learning to delegate, to build a strong but small team that has the same vision to expand and produce more merchandise in the future."

"I want to be an artist who continuously grows and is inspiring to others," Sarah says. "I wish one day I can open a physical store and have a free drawing workshop for those who want to learn."

- **WEBSITE/SHOP** *bigbearandbird.com*
- **INSTAGRAM** *@bigbearandbird*

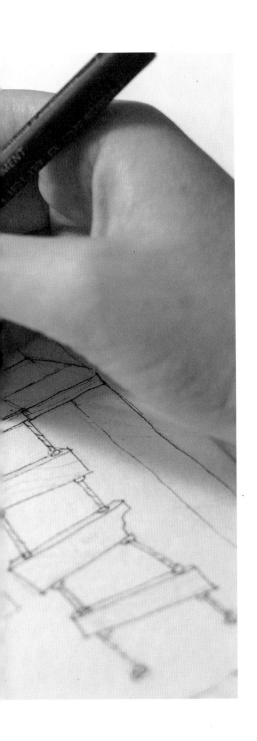

# SARAH MACNEILL

SHAWNIGAN LAKE, BRITISH
COLUMBIA, CANADA

"I am a visual thinker, an enthusiastic storyteller and a chronic night owl," says Sarah MacNeill. More specifically, Sarah has a degree in architecture from Dalhousie University, but currently works as a graphic designer, illustrator and photographer under her company name, Carte Studio. And if that is not enough, in 2009 she created another small craft-centric company called Koo & Poppet, making soft animal toys from Japanese linens and upcycled wool.

"I go about life with my husband and two spirited daughters in a house amid trees, near a lake on Vancouver Island," describes Sarah. "I dream about the energy of New York City, the allure of Paris and the style of Palm Springs on an hourly basis."

When Sarah started Koo & Poppet in 2009, she was part of an emerging group of professional crafters: new moms at home. With sites like Etsy and Poppytalk Handmade, she says, "we could be home with our babies, but also turn our creativity into something productive and sellable."

The Koo & Poppet family is made up of bunnies, bears, pigs, kittens, penguins, foxes and owls. "My background in architecture and current work as a graphic designer has influenced the design of the Koo & Poppet line in many ways," she explains. "I prefer a minimalist style, so I limit the material selection I work with to a few favourite fabrics that are chosen with great care. The design elements of each character are uncomplicated—usually nothing more than a tummy patch, muzzle or ear patches, and the faces are simple hand-stitched eyes and noses. Now and then, I add a whimsical feature like a custom appliqué of garden flowers or a bow on one ear. Even with such basic design, I like to think that I am able to capture a unique personality in each poppet."

Her dolls range in size from 11 inches to 19 inches tall and are made from wool fabrics, often upcycled wool skirts from thrift stores mixed with Japanese linens. They are stuffed with eco-fill poly stuffing, with the characters'

personalities coming alive through hand-stitched elements. Sarah also creates a bit of their story: "The characters are one of a kind and come with a name, a like and a dislike. For example, Cute Bunny Elliot likes drawing, but dislikes erasing." Each animal takes about an hour to make, she says, "less if I'm doing a big batch, assembly-line style."

Sarah can trace her love of making things back to childhood: "As a child I made collages out of magazine scraps, designed and sewed my own figure skating dresses, and listened earnestly as my dad taught me the fundamentals of photography through the lens of his Nikon SLR camera." Now as a mother, her own children, aged three and six, bring even more creative joy. "Their artwork is a huge inspiration to me. They take an uninhibited approach to drawing

and painting that I often lack. Their quirky personalities often inspire the characterization of Koo & Poppet characters."

In 2014, her characters came to life on the small screen in the form of an iOS app, through which Sarah realized a dream of seeing her work as illustrated animated art. "Developing an extensive body of illustrations for digital media felt like a major personal and professional goal achieved," she says. "The process was not without its obstacles, though. I've learned so much about business, partnership, communication and launching a product." Though the app has not yet performed as well as she had hoped, Sarah takes this in stride: "There is so much to be learned from a little failure," she says as she looks toward realizing the next dream: to write and illustrate a children's book. "I'd love to see Koo & Poppet become a wide world of lovable misfit characters for children—in hand, on screen and on the page."

With this ambition, Sarah touches on one of the most challenging aspects of living a life in craft: you can never abolish the to-do list. "One idea inspires another, and all the things you want to create seem like two lifetime's worth of work," she says.

Sarah works from a bright room in her home with a view of the backyard. The greenery often frames the rosy cheeks of her daughters as they break from their play outside and peek in to see what mom is up to. "I have a large built-in desk in my office with a computer on one end and a sewing machine on the other,"

Sarah explains. "I also use a separate table when drawing and designing a new concept by hand. I love white walls with art on them, so when I'm working I like to be surrounded by beautiful paintings, prints, posters and lettering. I've usually got a candle burning, music on and fresh flowers, too. And coffee, lots of coffee." Disliking clutter, she tries to keep it clean and tidy in order to maximize her productivity. "But sometimes it looks like a bomb went off," she admits.

With cute distractions like her daughters, getting in the zone and sustaining creative momentum can be tricky: "I tend to work best between the hours of 9 pm and midnight." Living a crafty and creative life is its own reward. "I'm motivated by the idea that anything is possible if you work hard and do your best. Impose no limits on your potential."

"The second you transition from making something for yourself or your loved ones to making something for the general public that they are paying for, many new factors come into play," notes Sarah. Placing a high value on customer service, quality craftsmanship, and attention to detail and presentation is vital for success. "I put a lot of energy into those aspects of the business because it's very important to me that my customers are completely happy with not just the product but also the experience of purchasing the product."

- **WEBSITE** cartestudio.com, kooandpoppet.com
- **TWITTER** @koo_and_poppet
- **INSTAGRAM** @carte_studio, @poppetsgame

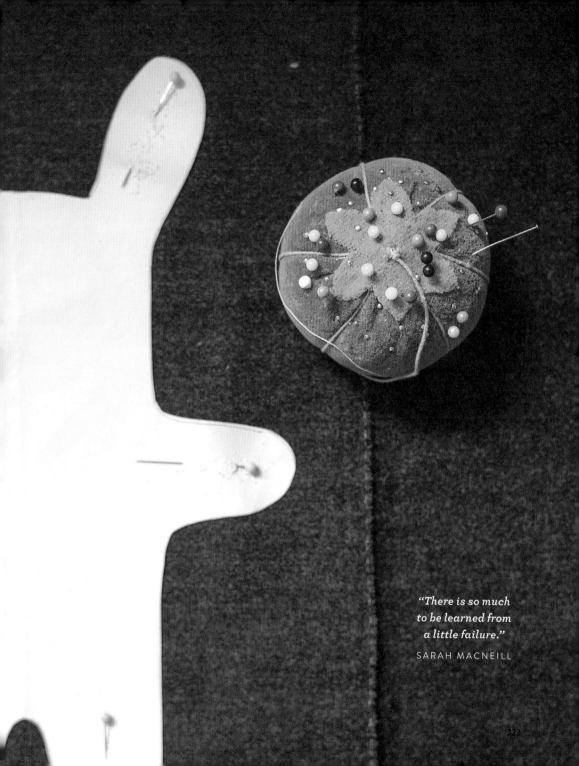

*"There is so much
to be learned from
a little failure."*

SARAH MACNEILL

# VIRGINIA GODAY

MEXICO CITY, MEXICO

Unlike many of the folks profiled in this book, Virginia Goday says she was not a very creative girl. "As a kid I was more drawn by numbers," she says, "and I dreamt about working in an office covered by papers and stamps." Virginia, who was born in a small city in Uruguay, looked up to her father, who was an accountant.

"My mother was more on the creative side and was always decorating our house and making crafts. She had a big loom covered with dust somewhere in the house." Virginia got a degree in economics and landed a job in a prestigious bank. "My life seemed pretty fine—I was living with my boyfriend and working in an office quite similar to the one I'd been dreaming of."

Virginia and her boyfriend went to Mexico for a vacation and he ended up getting a job in Mexico City. Virginia successfully applied for a scholarship at the university for a PhD pro-

gram in economics. "However, there was something inside of me that knew that something else was waiting for me out there," she says.

After three months in the program, she realized that her life had nothing to do with economics and her interests had shifted, rather dramatically: "I was dreaming about Mexican arts and crafts." With the support of her boyfriend, she signed up for every "artsy" class she could find. "I studied crochet, textile jewellery, sewing, felting and much more. I got a job in a design store but after a couple of years I decided to quit and attend a postgraduate course on textile design. That was when I fell in love with looms and the fabrics I was able to weave on them."

"After a while I could see that deep inside, I was always more connected with my mom and her creative side. It's just that it took me some time to realize it!"

A new job for her boyfriend took the couple to Boulder, Colorado, where Virginia purchased her first loom and started weaving cushions and scarves for sale. "I fell in love with Boulder, but after a couple of years my boyfriend—by then my husband—got a job offer in Mexico City and we came back," she says. "We've been living in Mexico City for the last two years."

Mexico City is large and chaotic, and Virginia appreciates her home studio: "I have my loom, serger and sewing machine among lots of threads and things that keep me inspired. I'm really grateful to get to work in my house and to not have to ride somewhere else every day." Her dog, Mina, keeps her company throughout the day.

The process of weaving fabric and then making products is long, but satisfying. "I usually start by browsing patterns that I like and sampling with different colours and threads," she explains. "I go to my favourite thread store in downtown Mexico City and pick up the colours that draw my attention. Next I think about what am I going to do with the fabric I'm about to weave. Depending on that I fix the width and length of the threads in my warp." Planning her design and setting up the loom can take a day or two, then the act of weaving can begin. "Depending on the length of my threads, it can take me from two to five days to finish

my fabric. It takes a lot of patience to see your work finished, but when you finally have it in your hands you know it's worth it. Once I have my fabric finished I sew the cushion, scarf or throw." For the more complex bags, her assistant Lupito helps with the sewing. "It would take me a lifetime to sew the bag properly!" she exclaims.

Although she admits that parts of the process are tedious, she enjoys the overall process. "Most of all I find it really amazing that out of some threads you can make something really beautiful," says Virginia. "There's something awesome about weaving; you never know how your fabric is going to look until you cut it out of the loom. That's my favourite part, the surprise effect."

*"I think there's a lot of people going back to their roots and trying to offer simpler products made by hand with antique techniques. People are tired of wearing the same industrialized stuff. Also there's a new awareness and appreciation for products that care for the environment and for the techniques used."*

VIRGINIA GODAY

At the moment, she sells her wares mainly through her Facebook page, but she admits that sales are not her strong suit: "My biggest challenge is to put a price on what I do. I want to give it all away as presents!" She would love to show her work in craft bazaars and textile exhibitions. "The fabrics I weave on my loom are one of a kind. I love to improvise as I'm weaving, so even if I wanted to, it's pretty hard to make two identical pieces." And therein lies the true beauty of things made by hand.

- **WEBSITE** *virtextiles.com*
- **INSTAGRAM** *@virtextiles*

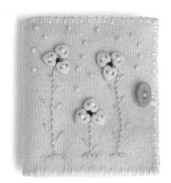

# SANDY KING

NANAIMO, BRITISH COLUMBIA, CANADA

Sandy King worked as a registered nurse for over 30 years. Once she retired from that profession and had the freedom and time to devote herself to something else, she returned to her roots and a love of creativity.

"I'm a grandmother of six who has just nicely settled into her sixth decade and I have maker genes," says Sandy from her home in Nanaimo. "I've been living life expressing myself in different creative ways for as long as I can remember—knitting, stitching, ceramics and woodworking, gardening and rug hooking, spinning and weaving, dyeing wool and basically anything I could do with my hands. I'm a maker."

Her love of making goes back to her childhood—when she was five, she asked Santa for a sewing machine. "The making and creating of things has been part of my life blood. I sewed clothes in high school and explored every expression of arts and crafts that trended along," Sandy says. These days she makes small decorated needle books, sketchbook covers and business card holders out of felt. "I let my imagination be the guide in the design. And when on a whim I added some buttons from my long-collected stash, it opened up another world of possibilities."

Sandy has noticed that things made by hand are having a resurgence in popularity. "I've been making things by hand for years. One of the challenges for us as makers of items that are long in man hours with relatively low remuneration for the skill is to keep going," she says. "It may not seem financially worthwhile to keep doing what we do. One-off items are time consuming, and sometimes the price we garner for time and effort isn't valued."

She also makes small, jointed teddy bears that she sells by word of mouth. An adventurous mouse named Wiston has become her companion and creative mascot: "Wiston is another expression of a character that has come through me—a combination of layers of skills I've amassed over the years." His muslin body is stuffed with polyester fibrefill and he has tiny glass beads weighing his hands, feet and body. She documents his adventures in the world, and creates his wardrobe—"his glasses and sunglasses out of gardening wire, his hiking boots out of leftover soft suede from the teddy bear making days." For others, Wiston functions as storyteller. "He's an ambassador for the creative spirit travelling the world, meeting and making new friends," explains Sandy. "He seeks wisdom with a curiosity about how to nurture our inner joy."

Sandy has a unique home studio in the family garage, a retreat that evolved out of necessity: "I started the process of carving out a space for myself in the family garage one year ago. I love having family and friends come to visit, but I found it frustrating to tidy up and then set up again once the company had left and the spare bedroom was mine once more. It just seemed logical to claim the garage, which was never used to park our cars. This way I can keep my supplies all together. I have more than one way of manifesting my creative expression, as you can tell, and I hate wasting valuable creativity time searching for something. I wanted a place to be able to find things quickly, make a mess and then walk away." With one-way glass, the garage is private but with lovely light shining in. "The added bonus is throwing the doors open in the good weather, to let the sunshine in and listen to the birds. In the winter I can cozy in and watch the rain pour down or watch the leaves whip around the yard in the wind through the glass doors."

Sandy has wholeheartedly embraced creativity in her life. "If I had a message to leave or an inspirational perspective to offer at my age, it would be that art matters," she says. "Making and creating by hand, by vision, is a gift to be shared and passed along. Out in the open, out of our studios, no matter how old we are or at what stage in life we are living. The making of things by hand still matters."

"I'm not sure what the future holds for me, but I will keep letting my inspiration come from the pockets of my life: my grandkids and my travels and my ever-present imagination and sense of humour."

- **BLOG** *sandymairart.wordpress.com*
- **SHOP** *sandymairart.etsy.com*
- **TWITTER** *@sandymairart*
- **INSTAGRAM** *@sandymairart*

"This kind of creative work becomes like a therapy for me."

ORIANA FREITAS

# ORIANA FREITAS

FUNCHAL, MADEIRA, PORTUGAL

Oriana Freitas lives on the small Portuguese island of Madeira, which is closer to the African coast of Morocco than its homeland. "I live with my husband and my two sons," says Oriana. "I began this life of craft in 2005, after I finished high school in sociology, in a pretty city called Évora, far away from home."

She lived for a year in Lisbon, where she was exposed to Portuguese artists and opened up a world of interest in curiosity in making things. "It became stronger and part of me, it's who I am. I'm happy creating things."

Returning to her home city was a difficult transition. A sense of loneliness at that time in her life fuelled a passion for amassing things like fabric, paper and collage—and vintage phones. "Returning to life on a island can be hard. I think this kind of creative work becomes like a therapy for me," she says. The creative process offers release and purpose.

"From my experience, remembering the context where I live and the reality I know, the most challenging thing about a life in craft is to be able to live only doing this, to pay your bills from it," she says. "The other challenge is to convince people that handmade work has value." With her country facing economic hardships and job loss, more people are turning to using their creativity to survive. "We see this in the last five years, more people doing things like selling things they make, and recycling more."

Oriana has a collection of old rotary phones, and is known locally for her unique styling of these objects. She recovers them in multi-patterned fabrics and notions, in essence decorating them with good memories of the simpler times that these phones evoke. "They were forgotten by society," she says. "Progress and technology put them in the basement." The analogue phones are still functional in Portugal, and quite literally represent connection over impossible distances.

Oriana counteracts geographic isolation with virtual connections: "My curiosity helps me a lot. Every day I find so many interesting people and their work around the world." It makes her feel, she says, like she is not alone "in this world of ideas." Oriana continues, "It's great to see that it is bigger than I imagine. I read magazines like *UPPERCASE* and *Flow* that never disappoint, read books, listen to music, look at nature through my window—this kind of lifestyle inspires me every day."

"My craft has become a part of me. I need it to feel fine, it makes my life become easier, more simple, more rich."

- **WEBSITE** *orianafreitas.wix.com/garotadocalhau*
- **SHOP** *ohsodaestudio.etsy.com*

# SARAH STEVENSON

"My design and architectural background has shown me that there is a distinct beauty in something made with your hands," says Sarah Stevenson from her home studio in Reno, Nevada. "It's a beauty that a machine cannot replicate. There is a polished skill that comes with years of perfecting your craft and this skill can not exist in a mass-produced environment."

Sarah received her design education some time ago, and she recalls when the ability to draw was a necessity: "We did not have programs to create for us. If you look back at the architectural drawings that existed before the computer age you will see that the documents were hand produced. These were an art form in and of themselves because each building was unique and each designer had their own style. Design school taught me to value the self-made over the commercial and showed me that handmade goods, though more time consuming, are an important way to hand down a talent and skill from generation to generation."

After 25 years as an interior designer, Sarah changed course to work on her own creative projects, mainly in mixed-media art, photography and creative events. Her professional background continues to inform her new path:

VIVIENNE MCMASTER

"I am lucky to be able to take all the lessons and skills I learned as a designer and use them to enhance my creative pursuits."

She uses photographs to design stationery and prints that are sold online as well as whole-sale. "I also create mixed-media art pieces that I show throughout the year, sell online and commission for editorial pieces," she says. Her photography expresses a love for travel, architecture and design. "I create my images for anyone who has a love for the excitement of travel and the intersection of all design dis-ciplines."

"I am learning every day about selling my work and about how the retail industry works. I nev-

er imagined that I would wholesale my artwork but I have found it has become an extension of my design background and I love developing new products along with the packaging to create my brand. I am constantly thinking of additional product lines I can create from my work and how I can blend my design background with my photography and art."

Sarah's creative community extends from a community of Instagram photographers to local artists to international artists. "I have found that my group is made of strong women with a definite sense of who they are, and who are always willing to share that with the world," she says. Sarah has nurtured these relationships by founding an art retreat for women called

create.explore.discover, which is celebrating its fifth anniversary. "I provide intimate gatherings where women can come and explore their own creative processes through day and weekend getaways."

"Both my mixed-media work and photography are based upon my story and my experience; as my own story grows and changes my work will grow and change along with it."

- **WEBSITE** *createexplorediscover.com*
- **WEBSITE/SHOP** *red-line-design.com*
- **BLOG** *red-line-design.com/blog*
- **TWITTER** *@redlinereno*
- **INSTAGRAM** *@redlinedesign*

# ROSALIND WYATT

LONDON, UNITED KINGDOM

"I went to a wonderful school where the emphasis was holistic: we learned Sanskrit, philosophy and meditation, geometry, Latin and Greek, as well as lots of art, music and drama alongside all the usual subjects," says Rosalind Wyatt. "I think this has given me a thirst for good things, and that can be tapped into from a diversity of sources and cultures. It has continued to grow and expand my view of the world and myself." This broad foundation taught Rosalind one important lesson: "There is only one way to live life: CREATIVELY!" The capitals and exclamation marks are Rosalind's own.

"Many teachers have helped and continue to help along the path—to them I owe everything," she says. Starting at home, Rosalind recalls her family's heritage and how it encouraged her creativity: "My mum is of Italian parentage, and though I never met many of her family, I'm sure these roots have given me an appreciation of family and a good life! She often tells me how one of her great aunts did fine embroidery work for couture fashion houses, and she herself made all our clothes, cooked fresh food and kept an amazing house and garden."

"My dad's family were Jewish tailors, but my dad took a different route. He worked for many years at the BBC, directing light drama, and now works as a voice coach. I really appreciate how my parents never dumbed things down for us kids. They took us to see Shakespeare and would take us to art exhibitions and festivals and concerts, and many of their friends were artists, which I loved. Dad would also show me old black-and-white movies, and musicals that he loved."

She has always loved stories, literature and theatre—for a time she thought she might become an actress—but took a visual route instead. "My mum loves to say how I learned to write with a calligraphy board and dip pen at age four," Rosalind says. "Apparently I loved the black ink!" When she discovered a degree course in calligraphy and bookbinding, she found something that encompassed all her interests and love of the humanities. "It ticked all the boxes for me: history, words, craft and the quietness of a working scriptorium!"

*"Inspiration is like the seasons—there are wonderful bursting spring times and, conversely, long cold winters! Through the changing seasons you have to keep going without getting caught in one particular groove."*

ROSALIND WYATT

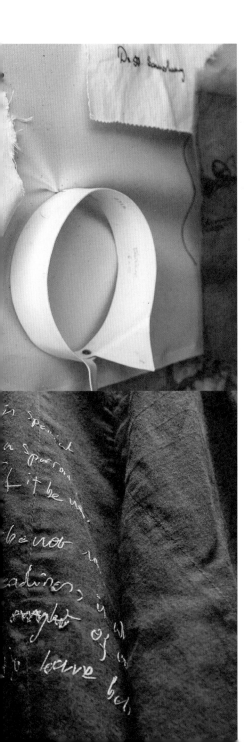

Rosalind's artwork—her stitching and calligraphy—is about words and letters, their sound and feel. "The choice of tool is uninhibited and relevant to the content of the text, therefore my range of writing tools has expanded from nib through to brush and now to a needle," she says.

"When you form a letter, something happens, and it is this 'something' that has kept me searching. I love the versatility of letters and the fact that within a single mark can be a thousand emotions."

"My recent work is exploring 'writing with a needle'—copying the handwriting of a letter into stitch. This is done directly by hand and eye onto a textile without pre-printing. I believe that handwriting reveals the personality of the letter writer. To me, it's like their voice after they've gone. I'm fascinated by all those unique details of a handwritten mark—the flow, rhythm and spacing that tell the story of a particular moment in time. When text and textile come together, that person and their story comes to life."

"I feel so blessed to be able to do what I do and to express myself in the way I do," says Rosalind. "When I stitch other people's stories, I find I naturally empathize with what they experience—stitch by stitch and moment by moment."

- **WEBSITE** *rosalindwyatt.com*
- **TWITTER** *@rosalindwyatt*
- **INSTAGRAM** *@artistrosalindwyatt*

# SHELLEY DAVIES

VICTORIA, BRITISH COLUMBIA,
CANADA

"In this age of dull digital images, we are craving the handmade, the homemade, the truly authentic," asserts collage artist and illustrator Shelley Davies. "I give voice to this need for authenticity with my collages, which show the hand's touch."

Shelley works out of her spare-bedroom studio in Victoria, British Columbia. With bookshelves overloaded with inspiring tomes, and her desk, made from an old door, nearly invisible under layers of scraps of paper, some might call her studio a mess. For Shelley it is the best way to create: "I embrace the chaos and something will percolate to the top of the pile and pleasantly surprise me."

She appreciates the accessibility of collage—"colourful bits of flotsam and jetsam," as she describes it—both as a technique for expression and as an inviting medium for the viewer. "Collage is a contemporary and universal medium to work in, and it's accessible to all.

No fancy materials required. I love that everyone can use such humble stuff and come up
with completely different and very personal
works of art." She starts with colour, usually in
a vibrant hue, taking a piece of paper or daub
of paint and starting to play by adding typographical scraps from collected ephemera or
bits of her own photographic prints—whatever
can create those happy accidents. She confesses to having a love affair with paper. "It always
comes from play, which translates into the finished art as pure joy."

Shelley recently mounted her first solo exhibition of her original collages and paintings, and
had some new stationery products on hand for
her customers. "People responded to the joy
and surprise in it, and had fun discovering all
the tiny details," she says. "They were very enthusiastic about my stationery, spurring me on
to create a line of products to share with them.
The line includes greeting cards, wrapping
paper, notebooks, prints and posters. Even
though my small stationery business is in its
infancy, I'm expecting it, too, along with my art
making, to be a playful evolution—learning as
I go, adding and subtracting, just as with my
collages."

- **WEBSITE** *shelleysdavies.com*
- **BLOG** *shelleysdavies.com/blog*
- **SHOP** *shelleysdavies.etsy.com*
- **TWITTER** *@ShelleyDavies9*

# SIOBHAN ROGERS

HUNTERS HILL, NEW SOUTH
WALES, AUSTRALIA

"I like to think a quilt is a hug you can't always give personally," says quilter Siobhan Rogers. "My quilts give the gift of comfort and warmth, and hours of my time have been poured into them." She likes to make quilts for family and friends for significant life events, whether it is a time when they need comfort, such as during an illness, or a time of celebration, like a marriage.

MATTHEW ROGERS

As a quilt designer, author and maker, quilts are piling up in her house. Even so, her children often claim new quilts even before they are off her machine. "I predominately create large quilts," says Siobhan. "I don't always mean to create such large-scale quilts. My designs draw lots of influence from large-scale geometric patterns—hence the large finished sizes—and I love my creations to be useful. My kids seem to prefer quilts that they can get lost in." Some quilts are kept for teaching purposes, while others are sold online.

Though her work is often put in the modern category of quilting, Siobhan sees her work fitting in with mid-century artists and even the quilters of the Depression. "It's taken me a long time to work out that I do indeed have my own style," she says. "My use of colour and my mix of linens, liberties [fabric by the famed UK brand Liberty] and commercial quilting fabrics seems to set me apart. Most students that come to my patchwork classes are wanting my input and opinion on fabric selections rather than sewing skills."

When it comes to sewing skills, she has a lifetime of practice, though she did train in photography and majored in social work in university. "Even as a child I made quilts. It was only as an adult with my own children that I realized that this was my art," she explains. "Quilting combines my love of fabric, my photographic eye and my love of styling and lifestyle design. I love what I'm doing and I have finally found my thing being involved in the quilting world."

The passion and facility for working with her hands seems to come from the generations before her: "I grew up with a father who excelled in woodwork and made musical instruments, and a mother who seemed to be good at anything she put her hands to—ceramics, leadlight glass, dressmaking, and she use to ink the skins on the drums that my father made in Celtic symbols. Both sets of my grandparents were also makers, more because they had to be. They were from a time when you didn't always have access to mass-produced items or money to spend. They took pride in the things they created."

Siobhan has a purpose-built quilting shed in the family's backyard, which she describes as "heavenly." "The previous owner of our house was a carpenter/builder and had built this fantastic shed in the backyard. When we moved in, it needed some major TLC, and my father rebuilt it for me. I have a bench built at the perfect height for me and lots of space. I bought a sewing table on wheels to make the space easy to change. I have one large white wall and one large black wall for my photography."

*"I have learned to price my work at what it's valued—I am not a mass-producing factory. My quilts are one of a kind. They take weeks to make and use lots of fabric."*

SIOBHAN ROGERS

With lots of simultaneous projects on the go, the shed is a patchwork of activities—from designing her next quilt for publication, working on a book for which she is also doing all the photography, or piecing a project. "I usually have three projects going at the same time. My concentration span for one project isn't great so I have to keep myself interested!" she laughs. "You have to keep in mind that I create a new quilt design every week or so. I am usually piecing a quilt sitting at my machine. When I have had an hour or so sitting at my machine I will get up and cut quilt two for a bit, and when my mind wanders I am usually sketching and pulling fabrics from my stash for quilt three. It keeps me moving around in my shed and keeps my mind going." Siobhan says having multiple things on the go is a boost to her creativity: "If I work on one project at a time I find I procrastinate."

- **WEBSITE/SHOP** *siobhanrogers.com.au*
- **BLOG** *beaspokequilts.blogspot.com.au*
- **TWITTER** *@BeaSpokeQuilts*
- **INSTAGRAM** *@siobhanrogers_beaspoke*

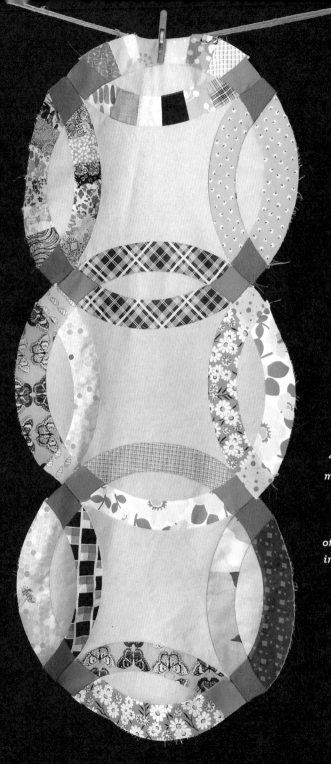

*"I see a magnificent movement of younger women taking up crafts and valuing its place. The work of individual artisans in arts and crafts has a huge following."*

SIOBHAN ROGERS

# SILVIA CASAS

MUNICH, BAVARIA, GERMANY

Originally from Spain, Silvia Casa moved to Munich, Germany, 10 years ago. Even though she comes from a big family with a long line of creative women, it was not until she experienced the long, cold German winters that her own creativity emerged.

"The 'crazy-creative-Silvia' woke up," she explains. "All of a sudden I needed to create and learn new things. I bought a camera and I learned photography. I started sewing, crocheting, knitting, quilting, experimented with calligraphy, hand-lettering, watercolours. All this made me start a blog as a place to show my tutorials and ideas, a place to be an inspiration for creative people. The most fun for me is using traditional techniques to make things with a modern and different touch."

To share what she was learning, she helped co-create a creativity club, "a meeting point for all creative Spanish-speaking people in Munich." The gatherings emphasize learning new things, and they serve to encourage and support the community. "We organize workshops of all different kinds of techniques—knitting, crocheting, stamp carving, embroidery—and other creative activities, like visiting craft fairs or other interesting events," she says.

The desire to facilitate creativity in others motivates Silvia in her own work: "I want to make things but also to be of service. I don't make or sell or teach stuff to become rich or to be famous; I want to teach or to sell my products to make people happy. I want my products to be the most beautifully made, and my courses the most interesting and fun, in order to make a difference, to make people happy, to infect people with the creativity virus. I want people to want to never stop learning and being creative, and I want to make them understand how happy they will be with it."

The quality of her photography that she shares on her blog is one example of her love of detail. She is an admitted perfectionist. "Photography is a very important part of my creative process," she says. "I always try to make sure that my tutorials have the most beautiful pictures."

"I love to make all different kinds of projects, especially with fabric. I love quilting, and I make a lot of modern, colourful quilts, but also smalls projects with fabric, paper or yarn, that can be easily made, even if you do not have any experience with making things by hand: from coasters to little fabric boats made to be placeholders, to yarn pompoms that make a flower bouquet. I show them on my blog, sometimes as easy tutorials, to be an inspiration for people who want to try easy projects and new things."

For now, the crafty part of her life is outside of a day job. "I would like to quit my job and make a living with my creativity activities, mainly selling my products—handmade and calligraphy—and giving workshops to children and adults," says Silvia. "It takes a lot of energy and time to be a crafter. Especially if you have a 9-to-5 job or other responsibilities, you might not always have the time, energy or motivation to also be a maker."

"My workspace is my happy place. I have a big table with my sewing machine, and a comfy chair. My books, yarns, fabrics, threads and buttons are close by, so I can reach them anytime. I have a mood board with beautiful pictures in front of me and always try to have

## THE REWARDS OF CRAFT
## BY SILVIA CASAS

Craft keeps you balanced—
it charges your batteries and
you feel fulfilled.

You are part of a great
community of people
around the world who are
motivated by great principles,
like beauty, learning or
preserving tradition.

Once you start learning,
the process never ends,
and you want to learn new
techniques and never stop
learning. Learning keeps us
young, happy and healthy,
independent of our age.

Last but not least, I love being
aware that craft activities connect
the past with the present.
They keep alive the traditions
and the great techniques that
our grandmothers (and their
grandmothers) used.

flowers on my table. It is not always tidy, but I love it even when it is a mess. And of course, music always accompanies me in my creative process."

Now that she is fully immersed in craft and creativity, Silvia can not imagine any other way of living: "I cannot imagine my life without making things. I cannot even sleep at night because of all the ideas that I have in my head. I absolutely love seeing and touching fabric, yarn and paper, and I enjoy working with them in a way that I cannot even describe. I positively believe that people who make things with their own hands have good souls. There is nothing that compares to a handmade or handwritten item. The love, the time, the energy invested can only transmit good things and make other people happy."

- **WEBSITE** *silvialagataconbotas.com*
- **SHOP** *lagataconbotas.etsy.com*
- **TWITTER** *@_Lagataconbotas*
- **INSTAGRAM** *@silvialagataconbotas*

# SUSSE LINTON

LONDON, UNITED KINGDOM

Susse Linton was born in Edinburgh, Scotland, and is half Scottish, half Danish. Her heritage and her talented family have been a big influence: "Although I was raised in Scotland I had a very Scandinavian upbringing, which has influenced my design work today. Growing up I was surrounded by creativity."

"School holidays were spent helping out at my father's architectural practice, and at my aunt's silversmithing workshop and store. Another aunt was a portrait painter, and I loved visiting her studio and the smell of oil paint when I was a a little girl. Both my mum and Danish grandmother really encouraged me to draw and paint and sew. All my Danish relatives were always knitting, sewing or making something. I was constantly making things as a child. My art teacher at high school encouraged me to take evening classes at art school, so at 15 I was enrolled in life drawing class and

367

knew then that I wanted to go to art college and lead a creative life."

Susse received a BA Honours degree in printed textiles from the Edinburgh College of Art and then studied for a postgraduate research diploma in textiles at the Winchester School of Art. "I ended up moving to London to freelance for various textile studios in London and around the world," she says. "I met my husband in London in 1998, and he encouraged me to set up my handbag collection, Susse Collection. I would make all the bags by hand and sell them to department stores and design boutiques around the world. My biggest market was in Japan; I visited Japan several times and worked on special commissioned projects for the Japanese department stores Mitsukoshi and Daimaru, and brands such as Shiseido. In 2005 my husband and I moved to Sydney, Australia, and there I started selling my bags online. Following the birth of my son in Australia, we moved back to London in 2010, where I now concentrate on creating surface patterns for all kinds of products."

It's fitting that Susse shares her studio with her husband, an animator. "I have always made things and been surrounded by family members who made things for a living," she says. "My space is very small so I have to be very organised with my supplies, and quite a lot of things live under my desk. I call it my telephone box studio. I do find working digitally helps in a small space. I need a clear space to think and work creatively." With a young child, they both find that the home studio "fits in with family life at the moment." When she needs interaction and learning with others, she finds it online. "Today I do find support with online communities, for example Lilla Rogers Studio School Bootcamp and Pattern Observer's textile design lab."

"My starting point is making artwork by hand, and then I turn that artwork into a surface pattern that can be applied to any surface or

product, whether it is paper, ceramics or textiles. I love the translation of my designs onto fabric, and how you can make textiles into three-dimensional objects. I target my designs toward women and children, and big kids like me." Her focus is on surface pattern design, an industry that has become more recognized of late, with more designers and illustrators aspiring to break into licensing. "I think today, the general public are surrounded by surface patterns, and they understand when you explain the function of surface pattern design. With digital technology it's much easier to cover any surface with a pattern. There are so many online courses and blogs about patterns, and sites like Society6 that make it so easy for artists to create a surface pattern to sell as a product."

"Many people who know me say they can recognize my style, they will say, 'It's very you, Susse.' I think my creativity is influenced by things that I find inspirational and love: I love travel, exploring new cultures, countries and cities. I also love mid-century design and design from the 1960s and 1970s, and I love vintage illustrations and also find them very inspiring—whether posters, graphics for packaging or children's illustrated books. I try to produce work that is positive, and that makes people feel uplifted and joyful."

"I can't go through a day without at least making a drawing or doing something creative. If I don't create something or make something or work on my designs, I feel like something is missing in my day. My passion for surface pattern has always come from a love of textiles. Pattern just adds so much needed colour and happiness into our world."

- WEBSITE *susse.co.uk*
- BLOG *sussecollection.blogspot.co.uk*
- SHOP *sussecollection.bigcartel.com*
- TWITTER *@sussecollection*
- INSTAGRAM *@sussecollection*

"I was finally saying to myself, go ahead, you have permission, your work is good enough, you have enough talent to make this happen. Deep down, I really believe that what I am doing and making is important and worthy of sharing."

STEPHANIE LEMAY

# STEPHANIE LEMAY

Stephanie Lemay's mother taught her to sew when she was five years old, and by age 14 she was working with a torch, making beads out of molten glass. Later, with a bachelor of fine arts degree in hot glass and printmaking and a master's in library science, Stephanie spent a number of years working at libraries and nonprofits, while teaching art and craft classes on the side and expanding her range of skills to include spinning yarn.

"I bought a wheel and soon had more yarn than I could knit or crochet myself, so I opened an Etsy shop," she says. Working under the name Rivulette, Stephanie started embroidering, making stitched textile collages, and spinning and making glassworks. "In June of 2014, I decided to leave my job and focus full time on my art and craft work."

"It took months of consideration before I jumped in and gave my notice but I'm so glad I did. It was incredibly freeing and took a huge investment in myself to take this step. I was finally saying to myself, go ahead, you have permission, your work is good enough, you have enough talent to make this happen. Deep down, I really believe that what I am doing and making is important and worthy of sharing."

Stephanie has continued her multi-disciplinary path. "I am excited about so many dif-

371

ferent things, but spend most of my time on textiles and fibres, and in the warm summer months I work outdoors with hot glass," she says. Her colourful Merino wools are perfect for knitting, crochet and weaving. "My yarns are usually self-striping, which means they knit or crochet into stripes without having to switch between different skeins of yarn."

Her recognizable yarns are her most popular offering. "I use a spectrum of colours, and my 32 Flavours yarn is an explosion of every colour imaginable. I make another yarn called Here n There, which is mostly white with stripes of colour thrown in at random. I feel like my artistic style is still developing, but I gravitate toward a delicate and detailed aesthetic with a bold use of colour. I appreciate the contrast of the two."

Her embroidery is done on linen and cotton, from which she makes jewellery pieces like brooches. "I'm also exploring the Japanese art of sashiko quilting and I love to find modern uses for it, like embellishing thrifted clothing," Stephanie says.

She continues to make glass beads with a torch and kiln, making one-of-a-kind pieces: "Only occasionally do I reproduce a piece or make a series of pieces that are related. My jewellery finds an audience with people who are looking for a high-quality special occasion piece."

With so many creative interests, Stephanie is interested in merging her techniques into a single piece, to build a body of work with a cohesive feel. "I've completed one piece of mixed-media textile collage that incorporates

374

quilting, embroidery, found objects and tiny beads. It's a piece of art that I envision hanging on a wall," she says. "I'm working on my second piece in this style now and it's about twice the size. A lot of time and consideration goes into making these pieces. There are weeks and months before I ever start cutting things out or working on layout that I'm just collecting. I go to flea markets, scour online shops, just keep my eyes open everywhere for fabrics, odds and ends, bits and pieces that I can incorporate. I was at the post office a couple weeks ago and I told someone about my work. She later gave me a bag of old lace and embroidered linens that she was getting rid of and it was all wonderful stuff, perfect for my work."

"I want to continue experimenting with ways to combine various media and techniques. I would like to explore the divide between art and craft, between fine art and decoration."

- **WEBSITE** *rivulette.com*
- **BLOG** *rivulette.com/blog*
- **SHOP** *rivulettecraft.etsy.com*

## ON ETSY AND SELLING

Stephanie sells her work on Etsy, which has its benefits and challenges. With such a vast platform, she experiences what most sellers do when they are just starting out: "I sometimes feel lost in the shuffle and it's difficult to stand out."

"There are challenges at first when it comes to cash flow, which is why it's helpful to have savings, a partner with a steady job, or a popular product that many people will want to buy right off the bat." Stephanie advises makers to schedule their time carefully and to make sure that marketing, research and customer service are part of their routine.

When it comes to selling, one must also have confidence and a thick skin. "I've found that I can be my biggest obstacle," acknowledges Stephanie. "I sometimes fear that my work will not be warmly received or people just won't get it. I am a worrier and this gets in my way sometimes." Recognizing our own weakness, says Stephanie, is the first step in overcoming it: "When I notice this happening, I take a small step like posting something that inspires me on my blog or listing a new item in my Etsy shop. The responses I receive from a small action like this encourage me to do more."

"The most rewarding thing about a life in craft is the satisfaction of knowing I'm doing what brings me the most joy in life. When I share my creative work with the world and people notice and commend it, I feel so proud."

378

# SOIZIC GILIBERT

PLOUGOUMELEN, FRANCE

"Creating is my way of thinking; I express the things I have inside me." With this statement, Soizic Gilibert gets to the heart of why we draw, paint, make and craft.

Having studied applied arts in Paris some 20 years ago, Soizic has a career of professional creativity behind her. She worked as a stylist for children's fashion and as a fashion designer for children's garments. "Strangely, the hard world of business in general, especially fashion companies, have shaped my creativity," she says. "As long as I worked as a stylist I had the feeling of being a little bit frustrated, but it gave me a rigorous method of working and creating. When I gave up the stylist work I kept this rigour but added some oxygen. And I love this mix."

In 2008, she shifted her career focus to textile design for home and fashion—and to allow more room for another of her loves, engraving: "As a textile designer I have a special style because I have to think of product, a sort of commercial style. Engraving is a free zone of creation where I can be myself."

Using an engraving technique called *pointe sèche*, she uses a very sharp tool to draw into plexiglass. "I put some special oil ink on my glass. Then I polish my plexi with a special fabric called a tarlatan. Finally, I use a press to print my design," Soizic explains. "For each print I have to put on some ink again and polish again." Though one might assume that polishing the plexiglass is routine, this is another stage in the process where Soizic can inject her personality. "I have a special way of polishing my plexiglass and it gives a special feel to my work"—so much so that people can recognize her work by the quality this process adds.

"My favourite subjects are trees, birds, houses, clouds and fish—among plenty of others," she declares. "I often incorporate some collages in my prints. These collages are made of printed

paper I made myself, directly inspired from my textile design work. It creates a link between these two areas, and it's quite important for me. Sometimes I work on the final prints with aquarelle pencils."

She sells her prints in art galleries, in the public library, at artist fairs and even from home. "They are made just to be nice to look at, to attract your attention and to let you think about the world behind them," she says.

Soizic lives in Brittany, in the west of France, a region she says is "very rich in creation." She is part of a group of engravers with whom she occasionally shares a studio. "I have a place with my engraver friends, big and warm with a big press and trees in front of the windows. We sometimes work together, to exchange our techniques, to drink tea or a glass of wine." She also has a workspace at home, about 15 square metres full of everything one needs to be inspired: books, tables, tools, pencils, brushes, computers, wood shelves and a little press. "It also has big windows and trees in front," she says.

Like the multiple possibilities that printmaking allows, so a career in creativity is full of options. Soizic is heartened to know that it is possible to have so much fun pursuing personal projects and still make a life from it. "I always want to do new things," she says. "One engraving brings me to another. It is, in a way, as if I could tell a story with no end."

- **WEBSITE** *soizicgilibert.com*
- **BLOG** *soizicgilibert.canalblog.com*

"I always want to do new things.
One engraving brings me to another.
It is, in a way, as if I could tell
a story with no end."

SOIZIC GILIBERT

SUBSCRIBE TO UPPERCASE MAGAZINE

uppercasemagazine.com